A Short History of China

Other Pocket Essentials by this author:

A Short History of Europe
A Short History of Africa

A Short History of China

From Ancient Dynasties to Economic Powerhouse

GORDON KERR

POCKET ESSENTIALS

First published in 2013 by Pocket Essentials,
an imprint of Oldcastle Books Ltd,
P.O.Box 394, Harpenden, Herts, AL5 1XJ
www.pocketessentials.com

Editor: Nick Rennison

© Gordon Kerr 2013

A CIP catalogue record for this book is available from the British Library.

ISBN
978-1-84243-968-5 (print)
978-1-84243-969-2 (epub)
978-1-84243-970-8 (kindle)
978-1-84243-961-6 (pdf)

2 4 6 8 10 9 7 5 3

Typeset by Avocet Typeset, Chilton, Aylesbury, Bucks, HP18 9FG
in 9.25pt Univers Light
Printed and bound by CPI Group (UK) Ltd, Croydon, CR0 4YY
For more about Crime Fiction go to www.crimetime.co.uk / @crimetime.uk

For my brother, Bill Kerr

Acknowledgements

My thanks go to Ion Mills and his team at Pocket Essentials for giving me the opportunity to work on this series of short histories, one of the most rewarding projects on which I have ever had the privilege to work. Thanks also to my indomitable editor, Nick Rennison, one of the nicest men in the world of books. Above all, though, I would like to thank my wife, Diane, who provides such generous and ungrudging support for all that I do.

Contents

Introduction

China, with four millennia of continuous history, is one of the world's oldest civilisations as well as one of the best documented. Its history was being written as early as the Shang Dynasty (c. 1700–1046 BC) and in the two great historical works, the *Records of the Grand Historian and the Bamboo Annals*, a dynasty – the Xia – that existed even before the Shang is also recorded. Its political system is handily broken up into hereditary monarchies known as dynasties that prevailed until the fall of the Qing Dynasty in 1911 and the first stirrings of a Republic of China.

Until that date, there were 557 emperors. Some were enlightened, cultured and humane men, but others have gone down in history as ruthless, cruel and dissolute. They were also often incompetent, a disaster for a nation that was dependent on the ability of the emperor to raise taxes fairly and efficiently as well as to exercise control over the bureaucratic elite that was a thorn in the side for so many occupants of the Dragon Throne.

China has often been blighted by the influence and ambition of foreigners, whether the marauding hordes from the steppe beyond the Great Wall to the north or the avaricious nations – Germany, Britain, France and Japan – of recent centuries, hungrily aspiring to carve China up between them. The elements, too, have played their part – flood and famine were for many centuries a part of the natural cycle in China, despite the efforts of many clever men to control the floodwaters and to dam the great rivers.

Nonetheless, Chinese culture has always managed to survive, even through the darkest times. One can only wonder at the way that Han Dynasty scholars reconstructed the Confucian classics from memory after they had been destroyed by the previous Qin

Dynasty many decades previously. The culture survived in this doggedly stubborn way partly because of the extraordinary conviction of the Chinese people that their land is the centre of everything – the Middle Kingdom, or 'All Under Heaven', as they describe it. Even when engaged in desperate decades-long warfare, they remained united by the fact that they were Han Chinese and they always strove to re-unite, to make their empire whole again.

For many centuries, the sophistication of the culture, science and technology of China left the West lagging far behind, the inventions and advances simply staggering and well in advance of similar innovations in the West. To the Chinese can be attributed the invention of the compass, gunpowder and – several centuries before Johannes Gutenberg – both woodblock and movable type in printing. Papermaking was first developed in China, leading to the first government-issued paper money during the Song Dynasty (960–1279). In the fifth century BC, the Chinese were using advanced metallurgic technology, including the blast furnace and the cupola furnace. They invented the escapement mechanism in water-powered clockworks in the eighth century and the endless power-transmitting chain drive in the eleventh century. The list is endless with advances in music theory, mathematics and astronomy thrown in for good measure.

In the background, however, was the constant cut and thrust of China's extraordinary dynastic history, centuries of peace followed by centuries of unimaginable turmoil, emperors murdered by their sons, or imperial hopefuls dispatched by ambitious dowager empresses. The death tolls were often staggering, demonstrating not only a disdain for human life but also the vast and inexhaustible supply of manpower that has always characterised China.

Ultimately, one cannot fail to be impressed and excited by a history at once strange and thrilling, to be appalled and captivated by the powerful men and women who sought control of the Middle Kingdom or who worked to make it a better place. As the new China emerges as a global superpower at the start of the twenty-first century, it is an appropriate moment to discover the fascinating history that has brought it to this point and to bear in mind the prescient words of Napoleon Bonaparte: 'Let China sleep, for when she awakes, she will shake the world.'

Note: This book uses the *pinyin* system, adopted as the international standard in 1982, for proper nouns. Where deemed necessary for clarification, place names are accompanied by their modern equivalents.

1. Geography of the Middle Kingdom

China is the third largest country in the world, measuring more than 5,200 kilometres from east to west and more than 5,500 kilometres from north to south. This huge expanse of land is stitched together by mountain ranges that form barriers between habitable river valleys. Dominating this land mass are two great river systems – the Yellow River to the north and the Yangtze River in the centre.

The Yellow River rises in the Bayan Har Mountains in Qinghai Province in western China and flows through nine Chinese provinces. It traverses the northern deserts before flowing south through a hilly area of fertile soil perfectly suited to cultivation. At the end of these highlands, the river turns to the east, now yellow from the silt it carries, its banks wide apart, and crosses the alluvial plain before emptying into the Bohai Sea. Often called 'the cradle of Chinese civilisation', it cuts across the Wei valley to the west of Beijing, an area considered the birthplace of ancient Chinese cultures and a region of great prosperity in early Chinese history. The Yangtze, Asia's longest river, carries a greater volume of water than the Yellow River. It rises in the glaciers of the Qinghai-Tibet Plateau, flows eastwards across southwest, central and eastern China and into the East China Sea at Shanghai. Its river basin is home to around a third of the population of the People's Republic of China.

Naturally, the regions through which these rivers flow differ greatly in every way. In the north, the temperature is colder and the terrain is flatter and more arid. It has a shorter growing season and alkaline soil in which crops such as wheat and millet flourish. The area north of the Yellow River does not enjoy sufficient rainfall for agriculture without irrigation. The silt collected by the river builds up the height of the riverbed, rendering the Yellow River prone to flooding and farmers and governments have, over the centuries, built dykes to maintain the course of the water. Nonetheless, floods, when they occur, are devastating, inundating vast swathes of land. Around the Yangtze, the weather is warmer and wetter, its annual rainfall of more than sixty inches making it especially suited to the cultivation of rice and the practice of double-cropping. The navigability of much of the Yangtze has made travel by boat more common in the south than the north.

Great physical features separate China from the world. To the north lies the steppe, the grassy plains of Inner Asia that stretch across Eurasia to the Ukraine and where animal husbandry is more successful than crop cultivation. These regions are populated by the traditional enemies of the Chinese – pastoralist peoples such as the Mongols and the Xiongnu. Arid deserts separate China from these lands. Meanwhile, to the west of south and central China lies the foreboding mountainous region of Tibet and to the southeast are forested mountain spurs and jungle. Off the coast are the South and East China Seas, sheltered by an arc of islands beyond which lies the Pacific Ocean.

This isolation was a significant factor in Chinese history and in the Chinese view of the world right up to the nineteenth century. For millennia, the Chinese thought of their land, bounded as it was by vast oceans, high mountains and infertile deserts, as 'All-Under-Heaven' (*tianxia*), the entirety of earth and the very centre of civilisation.

2. Neolithic Times and Early Empires

Prehistory

Early human beings – *Homo erectus* – first arrived on the Chinese subcontinent more than a million years ago, having spread during the Ice Age from Africa and west Asia. The best-known example of *Homo erectus* is Peking Man (*Sinanthropus pekinensis*), the name given to fossil remnants found in the 1920s and 1930s during excavations at Zhoukoudian, southwest of Beijing. It is now estimated that he may have lived as much as 680,000 or 780,000 years ago. The bones of forty-five men, women and children were discovered at Zhoukoudian, alongside evidence of tools. Peking Man was ape-like in appearance, but would have possessed basic speech skills and would have used his hands to manipulate objects. The remains were located in caves and it was in such places that he sought shelter. *Homo sapiens* – what we like to think of as modern human beings – arrived in East Asia about 100,000 years ago. Remains found in the Upper Cave at Zhoukoudian belong to a more advanced creature who lived about 50,000 years ago. His tool-making showed distinct improvement, the sharpness of the stone blades improved by a more efficient flaking method. Bone needles were now being used to sew hides to make clothing and these people hunted and fished but also gathered fruits, berries and edible roots.

By 5000 BC, Neolithic cultures had emerged in many of China's river valleys, practising agriculture, making pottery and textiles and living in village settlements. The development of agriculture had been facilitated by climate change, the weather becoming warmer and wetter. This led to more permanent settlements and social organisation. People were living in villages that consisted of pit dwellings, beehive-shaped huts made of mud and with reed roofs. Rice was being cultivated in the Yangtze valley region as early as 5000 BC and the diet would have been supplemented with fish and aquatic plants. In the north of the country where it was too cold and dry for rice cultivation, millet was the principal crop. It was during the Neolithic period that the domestication of animals began. At the time, woolly mammoths and wild horses could be found on the plains, while tigers and bears stalked the hills. Animals were hunted, some being killed for food while others were taken alive. Primitive man learned the skills of animal husbandry and dogs, pigs, sheep, cattle, chickens and horses were domesticated for practical purposes. Pottery for storage of food and drink was being made, most notably in the region of the Great Bend of the Yellow River (Huang He) where red clay pots decorated with purple or black lines have been found.

In the late Neolithic period, it is evident from the spread of pottery designs and shapes that different cultures were coming into contact with each other. This also, of course, led to conflict between communities. Metal began to be used to manufacture weapons and settlements were building defensive walls. It can be assumed that a hierarchy of sorts had developed by this time, with chieftains leading their men into battle. Religious elites were also emerging, evident in human sacrifice that was being carried out at the time. Captives would have been the victims of such rites, seen as a means of placating gods or ancestors or simply emphasising the power of the elites. Elaborate burials also demonstrate the fact that some individuals were more elevated socially than others.

Three Sovereigns and Five Emperors (c. 2852 BC to c. 2070 BC)

People gathered themselves into tribes or clans for protection and these clans allied with others in order to provide security against enemies for their herds, grazing lands, hunting grounds and settlements. From one such alliance emerged the legendary chieftain, Huangdi, also known as the Yellow Emperor who, according to tradition, reigned from 2697 to 2597 BC or 2696 to 2598 BC. Huangdi was one of the group of semi-mythological rulers and culture heroes known as the Three Sovereigns and Five Emperors who are said to have lived between about 2700 BC and 2100 BC. They were demigods whose magical powers, knowledge and innovations, according to tradition, helped China develop from a primitive to a sophisticated society. They are said to have lived to a great age and their rule brought a period of lasting peace. Details vary according to sources, but to Fu Xi, the Ox-tamer, was attributed the invention of the family and the domestication of animals; the invention of the plough and the hoe is credited to Shennong, the Divine Farmer; Nüwa, possibly the wife or sister of Fu Xi, is seen as the creator of mankind.

Huangdi, often referred to as the ancestor of the Huaxia race – the Chinese people – is said to have invented the bow and arrow and to have secured the plain of the Yellow River for his people. Tradition holds that he fought the first battle in Chinese history, the Battle of Banquan, sometime during the twenty-sixth century BC, a battle that is credited with the formation of the Huaxia tribe which was the basis for Han Chinese civilisation.

It was a time of transition as society moved from the Neolithic to the Bronze Age and metal implements and tools began to supplant stone ones. By this time, farming was well developed and farmers were using irrigation techniques to water their land. Silk was being made and wood was being used in the construction of houses. Transport, too, was developing with the use of carriages and boats and the first signs were emerging of efforts to create a written language.

Xia Dynasty (c. 2070 BC to c. 1600 BC)

Around 2000 BC a more sophisticated Bronze Age civilisation emerged. It domesticated the horse, used writing, worked metal and produced goods that led to a stratification of society, both political and religious, with some families becoming wealthy and powerful. One such was the Xia who are thought to have emerged towards the end of the third millennium BC as a ruling dynasty, the earliest to be described in such venerable ancient chronicles as *Zhushu Jinian* (*Bamboo Annals*), *Shujing* (*Book of Documents*) and *Shiji* (*Records of the Grand Historian*). The Xia would rule until midway through the second millennium before the birth of Christ. It is worth noting, however, that as China's first written system on a durable medium – the oracle bone script – was not devised until the thirteenth century BC, the existence of the Xia has yet to be proved by the only means available – archaeological investigation.

According to Chinese texts, the Xia dynasty was founded by Yu the Great (c. 2200–2100 BC), the grandson of Zhuanxu, one of the legendary Five Emperors. According to the legend of China's Great Flood, Yu's father, Gun, was ordered by King Yao (c. 2356–2255) to solve his kingdom's problems with flooding. For nine years, Gun built earthen dikes across the land designed to control the waters. But during a period of heavy flooding, the dikes collapsed and the project was deemed a failure. Gun was executed by King Shun who had succeeded Yao as ruler. Shun recruited Yu to take over from his father but instead of building more dikes, Yu dredged new river channels, to serve both as outlets for the torrential waters, and as irrigation conduits to farmlands some distance away. He worked at this task for thirteen years with the help of around 2,000 people and succeeded at last in containing and managing the flood waters.

Shang Dynasty (c. 1600 BC to c. 1046 BC)

In about the sixteenth century BC, the Xia were defeated by the neighbouring tribe, the Shang, a mainly agricultural people who went on to rule for almost six hundred years. King Tang of Shang (c. 1675 – c. 1646 BC) had been determined to bring an end to Xia rule and allied with neighbouring tribes to this end. He seized the throne and sent the last Xia ruler, Jie (c. 1728 – c. 1675 BC), into exile. The Shang did not hold sway over a very large part of China but their influence was far-reaching, their technology and decorative motifs being copied throughout the Yangtze valley.

During the Shang period, wheeled vehicles became increasingly common and horses began to be harnessed and used to pull war chariots and royal carriages. They were responsible for the invention of many musical instruments and Shang astronomers made observations about Mars and various comets. The Shang developed a system of writing that has been preserved on bronze inscriptions as well as on pottery, horn, jade and other stones. In particular, it has been found on oracle bones – turtle shells, the shoulder blades of cattle and other bones – which were used for divination. Thousands of these bones were discovered at the end of the nineteenth century near Anyang, one of the Shang's five capitals, providing vital information about the politics, economy and religion of the Shang and confirming as truth much of what had previously been regarded as legend or myth.

The Shang used bronze to make a wide array of implements and weapons, from sacrificial vessels to needles and spears. This led to a differentiation in types of labour and a more productive society. The surplus that was generated was used in trade and, as craftsmen congregated in specific areas, it encouraged the growth of urban communities. As in other fledgling societies, cowrie shells were used as currency. Shang cities were stoutly protected with walls made of beaten earth sometimes measuring more than fifty feet at their base.

Shang craftsmen made huge, highly decorated bronze ritual vessels and a great deal of the goods they manufactured, such as wine cups and weapons, are of unsurpassable quality. Slaves were used in the production of such items and they were also used in the construction of palaces for the Shang rulers and their families. When the ruler died, he was interred with items and even slaves – buried alive – whom, it was believed, he would need in the next world. Chariots and the skeletons of charioteers as well as countless priceless items made of jade, gold, bronze and stone have been excavated from such tombs. Their size is evidence of the power of the Shang rulers, their ability to engage sufficient numbers of workers to excavate holes up to forty feet deep, to construct immense burial chambers and to fill in the site afterwards with layers of compacted earth.

It was not just military supremacy that guaranteed a ruler his rank. He also served as a priest in the worship of the god Di and the royal ancestors. It was because he was the best placed person to communicate with these ancestors who in turn were best placed to communicate with Di, that he was felt to be a suitable ruler.

The Shang were undone by constant warfare against their enemies and oppression by their rulers of their slaves. During the decisive and bloody Battle of Muye, fought around 1046 BC, the Shang ruler's slaves transferred their allegiance to the enemy – King Wu of Zhou. The Shang were defeated and their last king, the cruel and oppressive Di Xin (also known as Zhou; ruled 1075–1046 BC), one of the most decadent of all Chinese rulers, committed suicide by setting fire to his palace.

Zhou Dynasty (1046 BC to 256 BC)

Western Zhou: c. 1046 BC to 770 BC

The Zhou period is the earliest from which texts have been handed down. The classic Confucian work, the *Book of Documents* (*Shujing*), claims to contain the Zhou version of their history, describing the defeat of the Shang as a victory over a decadent state led by a dissolute ruler. Initially an illiterate and fairly backward people, the Zhou assumed many of the practices and customs of the Shang, including their farming methods, their writing system and their facility with bronze. They would rule for 900 years and during that time there would be great change including an explosion of intellectual and artistic excellence.

King Wu died several years after his conquest of the Shang and was succeeded by his son, King Cheng (ruled 1042–21 BC), although his youth meant that a regent, the Duke of Zhou, had to be installed to rule in his place. The duke stamped out rebellion among the king's family and also added to the territory ruled by the Zhou.

The Zhou king was the sole source of authority and government. He kept his princes and nobles in line using feudal means – a system known as *fengjian* – by distributing estates to them. While they ruled independently within their own lands, they effectively became his vassals and had to protect him and his court if attacked. They paid tribute to their ruler and rendered homage to him in a strictly observed ritual.

During the Western Zhou, the dragon began to be a powerful symbol to the Chinese, signifying the water god and representing, therefore, the strength and fertility brought by rain. The dragon soon became the exclusive emblem of the ruler, his throne becoming known as the 'dragon throne'. The Duke of Zhou devised the 'Mandate of Heaven' doctrine that was to define Chinese dynastic rule. The ruler was called the 'Son of Heaven' and enjoyed the sole right to perform important rituals and offer sacrifices designed to guarantee the harmony of the seasons and the reliability of harvests. Thus, the Son of Heaven, expected to live a scrupulous life, would be held responsible for disasters and catastrophes such as bad harvests. It was thought that such events reflected on his moral probity and the Zhou believed that Heaven would withdraw its mandate from an evil ruler. This, they claimed, is what had happened in the case of the Shang.

The Zhou practised ancestor worship, believing that their dead ancestors had the power in heaven to wield influence over their descendants below. The protection they offered was in direct proportion to the quality of the sacrifices made to them. Sacrifices, however, could be made only by male family members, making it a disaster if a noble family had no surviving males to continue to placate the ancestors. The commoners, meanwhile, worshipped many deities, including the spirits of the rivers and the mountains, the Rain God, the Lord of Thunder and the Count of the Yellow River. Individual families had household gods and each village venerated its own god of the soil. Further peace, prosperity and contentment were available through the proper observance of funeral and mourning rituals, especially where parents were concerned.

Ancestor worship gradually spread to commoners, though, and they even began to assume surnames which had not been the case when the Zhou first seized power. Commoners, nonetheless, remained virtually slaves, obliged to till the land of their lord and pay him for the privilege. They grew wheat, maize, rice, sorghum, beans and a wide variety of other food crops and they planted fruit trees. Food was also obtained from hunting, while women were responsible for the management of silkworms. The success of agricultural production further encouraged the growth of urban life. Towns were filled with slave workers who had a much worse time of it than commoners, their master retaining the power of life and death over them. They were classified alongside cattle and, indeed, one Chinese word for slaves translates literally as 'animal people'.

Things were different, however, in the steppes of the more arid north where agriculture was not possible and people adapted to a nomadic way of life forced upon them by the need to move their herds to fresh pastures in summer and winter. These peoples were regarded by their southern neighbours as barbarians and there was conflict between the two for many centuries.

The twelfth and last king of the Western Zhou was King You (795–771 BC) whose accession was hardly auspicious, greeted as it was by an earthquake, landslides and eclipses of both the sun and the moon. You is said, however, to have paid little heed to such things and he created dissent amongst even the few who supported him by tampering with the succession to please his favourite concubine. He had also alienated his subjects by constantly summoning them to battle against imaginary invaders. Finally, when the nomadic Xianyun did launch an attack on the Zhou capital of Haojing, no one rallied to King You's call and he was killed. The majority of the Zhou nobles fled Haojing and the Wei River valley and established their base at the alternative capital to the east, Chengzhou, now the modern city of Luoyang. It was the beginning of the period known as the Eastern Zhou.

Eastern Zhou: 770 BC to 256 BC

The Eastern Zhou period, although a time of political instability and moral crisis, represented a crucial moment in the development of Chinese intellectual pursuits. The first half of the period is commonly known as the 'Spring and Autumn' period (c. 771 BC to

476 BC or, according to some sources, 403 BC) and it took place in the alluvial plain of the Yellow River, the Shandong Peninsula and the Huai and Han River valleys. Its name is derived from the *Spring and Autumn Annals* which chronicle the state of Lu between 722 and 481 BC, a work associated with the great Chinese teacher, editor, politician and philosopher, K'ung Fu-tzu, known to the West as Confucius (551–479 BC). The second half, lasting until 221 BC, has been given the name the 'Warring States' period because of the internal conflicts with which it was blighted, as described in the historical work, *Record of the Warring States*.

During this time, the vassal states grew stronger and the Zhou ruler's authority was increasingly challenged. Zhou kings retained only nominal power, their real control extending only to a small royal area around their capital, Luoyi, situated close to modern-day Luoyang. The senior feudal princes – known later as the twelve vassals – assembled for regular meetings at which important issues were discussed and often one of them was appointed to the position of commander of all the Zhou armies.

The period was characterised by the emergence of a new social group – scholars. They became useful to local princes as scribes as well as in advising them in the correct performance of ceremonies of state and religion and for tutoring their children. The earliest Chinese academies were created at this time, scholars and sages from other states attending establishments such as the Academy of the Gate of Chi. Thus, was control of education lost to the nobles and the priests as a class of *shih* – literati – evolved that would later become the mandarins, or bureaucrats, who ran China. *Shih* roamed from state to state offering their services and their advice to rulers. As time passed, smaller states were subsumed by the larger ones and some, such as Chu and Wu, declared independence from the rule of the Zhou.

Confucius

Amongst these wandering sages was a scholar named Confucius whose importance in Chinese history cannot be underestimated. Born into an aristocratic family that had seen better times, he founded the Ru school of thought and his teachings, which are preserved in the *Lunyu or Analects*, constitute the basis of much of subsequent Chinese thinking on the education and comportment of the ideal man. They included advice on how he should live and interact with others and detail the types of society and government in which he should participate.

Much of what is said about the life of Confucius should be regarded as legendary, rather than factual. Many of these legends were included in the *Records of the Grand Historian* (*Shiji*) written by the Han dynasty court historian, Sima Qian (145 – c. 85 BC) at the end of the second century BC. Confucius, he wrote, had endured a poverty-stricken childhood and, on reaching manhood, had been forced to work as an accountant and even as a cattle herder. We have no idea how he was educated although tradition holds that he studied ritual with the Daoist master, Lao Dan, music with Chang Hong and the lute with music-master Xiang.

In middle age, he, too, began to teach, gathering around him a group of disciples. He also began to involve himself in politics in Lu – in today's Shangdong province – where he lived. Duke Ding of Lu (ruled 509–495 BC) appointed the 50-year-old Confucius Minister of Public Works before making him Minister of Crime. For some reason, however, he was forced to leave office and is said to have gone into exile, although exile and suffering are regular themes in the lives of early Chinese heroic figures. Confucius is said to have left Lu with many of his followers and journeyed in the states of Wei, Song, Chen, Cai and Chu in search of a ruler willing to employ him and use his talents. During this period, he is said to have endured great hardship and danger.

In 484 BC, he returned to Lu where he spent the remainder of his life teaching, editing the *Book of Songs* – an anthology of ritual hymns, heroic verses and pastoral odes – the *Book of Documents* and other ancient classics including the *Spring and Autumn Annals*, the court chronicle of Lu. Sima Qian reports that, 'In his later years, Confucius delighted in the *Yi Jing*, the divination manual that remains popular both in the East and the West to this day. These works became known as 'Confucian Classics' and led to Confucius being viewed as the spiritual ancestor of later Chinese teachers, philosophers, historians and literary scholars.

It is in the *Analects* that we find the best notion of what exactly the teachings of Confucius constituted. A collection of sayings of the master, assembled by his disciples, the *Analects* shows a thinker who respected the early days of the Zhou, disdaining the disorder and instability of the time in which he lived. He revered the cult of Heaven and ancestor worship that he believed were manifestations of a golden age in Chinese history. Indeed, such a view was shared by countless rebels and reformers in China until as late as the nineteenth century.

His main focus, however, was on social relations and the proper conduct of human affairs. He advocated the duties of humans to the living, not the dead, and championed a doctrine of benevolence – the concept of *ren* – or love for one another in phrases such as 'What you do not wish for yourself do not do to others.' He argued that men are responsible for their actions, that we can do little to alter our fated span of existence, but we are the ones who determine what we achieve during that time and what we are remembered for. He also emphasised the need for strict rules of behaviour, especially regarding that of inferiors to superiors. Family hierarchy was important, he claimed, and should be strictly observed. Thus, should the son obey the father, the younger brother should obey the older brother and the wife should obey the husband. Furthermore, the subject should absolutely obey the ruler, in the same way that the Son of Heaven displayed obedience to Heaven.

In family matters, Confucius advocated that authority should be held by the aged and with the males. Women did not really benefit from his teachings. Marriage was a question of family arrangement and not love and the objective was the survival of the family and the family name. On marriage, a young woman left her own family and moved in with her spouse's family, remaining with them even if her husband died. The attitude towards women can be seen in a number of verses in the *Book of Songs*:

Sons shall be born to him –
They will be put to sleep on couches;
They will be clothed in robes

Daughters shall be born to him –
They will be put to sleep on the ground
They will be clothed in wrappers

Confucius prescribed ritual and etiquette – *li* – for every occasion and although they may seem like empty formalities to us, they seemed significant and useful at a time during which social relationships were being damaged and respect for authority was diminishing. Expressing respect for superiors through such acts and rites showed an individual to be worthy of respect and admiration. Of particular interest to Confucius was the proper behaviour of a 'gentleman' right down to the appropriate way to dress:

'A gentleman does not wear facings of purple or mauve, nor in undress does he use pink or purple. In hot weather he wears an unlined gown of fine thread loosely woven, but puts on an outside garment before going out of doors. With a black robe he wears black lambskin; with a robe of undyed silk, fawn. With a yellow robe, fox fur. On his undress robe the fur cuffs are long; but the right is shorter than the left. His bedclothes must be half as long again as a man's height... Apart from his court apron, all his skirts are wider at the bottom than at the waist.' *Analects*, Chapter 10.

Many believe writings such as these to be descriptions of the daily life and comportment of Confucius himself but, in instructions such as bowing twice when seeing a messenger off or avoiding lying in the posture of a corpse in bed, he established the model of courtliness and personal decorum that guided countless generations of Chinese officials.

Confucius extended his doctrine to rulers, too, encouraging them to be considerate of the welfare of their people and never to take them for granted or exploit them. Good government, he claimed, kept men happy and maintained order. 'Govern the people by regulations,' he wrote. 'Keep order among them by chastisements and they will flee from you, and lose all self-respect. Govern them by moral force, keep order among them by ritual and they will keep their self-respect and come to you of their own accord.'

By the fourth century BC, Confucius was being revered as a great sage, the Chinese philosopher, Mencius, saying of him, 'Ever since man came into this world, there has never been one greater than Confucius.' In centuries to come, scholars would commit his entire oeuvre to memory and Confucianism would become the orthodox doctrine of state. In the time in which he lived, however, conflict between states escalated and in 479 BC, the year in which the great sage died, the state of Chen was annexed by its neighbour Chu, marking the start of the period known as the Warring States.

Warring States: 476 BC to 221 BC

Following the move of the Zhou to the east, the rulers never really succeeded in re-establishing control over their vassals and China entered a period when the influence of the central authority was diminished. Although Zhou kings were still regarded as Sons of Heaven and, consequently, intermediaries with Heaven, they had lost their military power, their armies often weaker than those of the princes they supposedly ruled. By 335 BC, many of the regional lords had begun to style themselves 'king', rejecting the authority of the Son of Heaven. The 148 states that had emerged were gradually subsumed by the larger and more powerful ones until finally only seven remained – Qin, Han, Wei, Zhao, Qi, Chu and Yan. These would become the Warring States after which this violent period was known. However, despite the turbulence of the times, there were advances.

The earliest cast iron artefacts date to the fifth century BC China, in what is now Luhe County in Jiangsu, an east coast province. Iron was used for making weapons, agricultural implements – especially the iron plough – and for building. Control of flooding of the Yellow River and other waterways brought great benefits to many states and improved irrigation techniques also helped. More land was cleared for cultivation and harvests increased, providing grain surpluses that could be used for commerce and to support even more people not working on the land such as merchants and craftsmen who lived in towns and cities. During this time, too, the cowrie shell became inadequate as a unit of currency and people began to fashion replicas of them in bone, stone and bronze. Eventually, the use of metal coinage became common and there were the first stirrings of a money economy.

Metal tools and implements became valuable items and soon small replicas of them were being used as tokens of exchange, developing into 'spade' and 'knife' coins. Later in the period, round coins were first brought into use, made of cast bronze with a hole in the middle to enable them to be strung together. The characteristic Chinese eating implement, the chopstick, also started being used around this time. For protection of both people and the store of surplus grain held in large granaries, towns began to be surrounded by defensive walls. The invention of the crossbow had changed the nature of warfare, of which, at this time, there was a great deal. In earlier times, battles had been fought by nobles in war chariots, but now archers on horseback lined up against each other. Harvest surpluses also meant that standing armies could be supported, mainly drawn from the ranks of the peasantry. Several northern states learned the lessons of their nomadic neighbours and added cavalry to their armies. This had the unexpected effect of changing Chinese fashion. Until then, the long skirt had been worn, but horse-riding demanded trousers and they became the mode of dress for all.

The Hundred Schools of Thought
Perhaps it was the centuries of continuous warfare and social upheaval that made Chinese thinkers begin to question the nature of existence giving rise to the phenomenon known as the Hundred

Schools of Thought. As ever in China, the number 'Hundred' in the title is not to be taken literally; it merely signifies that there were many.

Daoism was perhaps the most influential school of thought after Confucianism. The Daoist classic, the *Dao De Jing* (*Classic of the Way and Its Power*) is a poetic, elliptical masterpiece, traditionally ascribed to Laozi (also known as Lao Tzu – 'Old Master'), a record-keeper at the Zhou court, who lived in the sixth century BC. However, the work was, in all likelihood, compiled in the third century BC using the ideas of a number of sages. In contrast to the practicalities of the Confucian view of life, the Daoists adopted a mystical approach. Civilisation was to them the source of all suffering. They advocated a return to 'natural' simplicity and natural harmony. The world created by man was bad, as were its institutions, human ambition and the struggle for improvement. Passivity was the way to avoid such evils. Happiness and tranquillity could be achieved only by following the *Dao*, the 'Way' of nature. They taught compassion, humility and the avoidance of selfish behaviour and some Daoists even withdrew completely from society in pursuit of their doctrine of 'quietism'. The question of death became important to later Daoists and they embarked upon a quest to find the elixir of life, a search that led to many important scientific discoveries.

Mohists were followers of Mozi (c. 470 – c. 391 BC) who believed in universal love, irrespective of family and rank, in direct opposition to what Confucius had advocated. Government, Mozi believed, should be carried out by men of ability and moral probity rather than by rulers decided by heredity. Mohists condemned the fact that some lived in luxury while others had insufficient food and clothing.

The philosopher Meng Zi, known to the West as Mencius (c. 370 – c. 300 BC), had been a student of the grandson of Confucius and, like the great master, he travelled amongst the various states offering his services to their rulers. According to Mencius, human nature is inherently good, but is corrupted by society. His view of social hierarchy was prevalent amongst the Chinese upper class into the twentieth century. Society, he said, was made up of two complementary groups – the 'superior' men, those of the ruling class and the 'mean' men, who were meant to be ruled. This helped to initiate contempt amongst intellectuals for the working classes and only in the upheaval of the twentieth century was it eradicated. At the time, and ever since, however, the part of Chinese society that was ruled has been separated into three distinct segments. Farmers were regarded as the foundation of society and enjoyed the greatest status among the ruled; merchants enjoyed less respect, viewed as non-productive and living off the work of others; and soldiers, often viewed in other societies as something of an elite, enjoyed little respect in Chinese society and were regarded as outsiders.

At the opposite end of the spectrum from Meng Zi was Xunzi (c. 312–230 BC) who believed that man is inherently evil and that observance of ritual, training and education was required to curb his evil tendencies. He also believed in strong, authoritarian government.

Legalists also believed that man's nature is essentially evil and that only the rule of law can restrain it. They advocated, therefore, a strong, centralised and absolute state. Repression was justified, they argued, and hereditary rulers were required to create a strong state. Everyone in the state should do productive work, they said, and the teaching of music, philosophy and history was corrupting. The leader of this school of thought was Han Fei (c. 280–233 BC), a prince of the Han state, who believed that military power and productive agriculture were essential to the well-being of a successful state. Interestingly, his philosophy enjoyed renewed interest during Mao Zedong's leadership of China.

There were many other schools of thought that reflected the astonishing intellectual vitality of the late Zhou. Utopians, hermits, agriculturalists all emerged with ideas as to how life should be lived. Given the warfare that formed a background to all this philosophising, it is little surprise to learn that military affairs also attracted theorists. The famous *Art of War*, attributed to Sun Tzu (c. 544 – c. 496), a contemporary of Confucius and a high ranking military general, became the definitive work on military strategy and tactics of its time and influences military thinking as well as business tactics and legal strategy in both the East and the West to this day.

Qin Dynasty (221 to 207 BC)

The First Emperor

One of the states that began to consolidate its powerbase during the Warring States period was Qin. Situated in the northwest, around the Wei river valley, it had prospered through improved irrigation. It had also learned lessons from the neighbouring nomads and had introduced cavalry into its army. In 361 BC, Shang Yang (390–338 BC), a leader of the Legalist school of thought, was appointed chief minister to the ruler of Qin. Yang enacted numerous reforms in accordance with his philosophy, converting Qin from an insignificant state into a powerful militarised and centralised kingdom. He reduced the influence of the old aristocratic families, replacing them with a new military elite. Appointments were made based on military success and the entire nation was militarised.

Everyone, no matter their rank, had to work in agriculture or weaving and only by producing a large quantity of grain or silk could a person be exempted from forced labour. The lazy, the work-shy and those who tried to gain from other occupations were enslaved. Although harsh, these reforms were undoubtedly successful and the state of Qin increased in power, its armies representing a serious threat to the other six states. The danger, of course, was that the others would join forces against their common enemy, but the Qin ensured by diplomacy as well as military force that this did not come to pass. Gradually, Qin annexed the other states of Han, Zhao, Wei, Chu, Yan and Qi. By 221 BC the Middle Kingdom was unified under one ruler – King Zheng – and a powerful central government. He took the name Qin Shi Huangdi (First Emperor) and ruled 'All-Under-Heaven' until his death in 210 BC. It was a pivotal moment, marking the end of the Warring States Period and heralding the establishment of the first centralised empire in Chinese history. Two thousand years of imperial rule began.

A government was set up at the capital of the newly united state,

Xianyang (near the modern city of Xi'an in Shaanxi province), and the emperor began to exercise autocratic rule. Repressive measures designed to quell opposition were enacted by his Legalist chief minister, Li Si (c. 280–208 BC) and standardisation was introduced in weights, measures and writing. Opponents of Legalism – followers of Confucianism amongst them – were persecuted.

The empire was ruled by non-aristocratic officials whose positions were not hereditary and feudalism disappeared, the estates of the lords being appropriated by the state. The country was divided into 36 provinces and within these were counties, all under the direct control of government-appointed governors and officials. These officials provided the centre with tax revenue and were also responsible for conscripting men for army service or public projects where their labour was needed. Private possession of arms was made illegal in order to prevent local leaders from organising rebellions and several hundred thousand prominent families from the defeated states were forced to move to Xianyang so that the emperor could keep an eye on them. Education was strictly controlled, restricted only to the training of officials. All writings, apart from manuals on such topics as agriculture and medicine, were burned and legend has it that 460 scholars were buried alive as a warning to others.

A census of the entire country was carried out, a remarkable twelve centuries before England's first initiative of this kind – the Domesday survey. The main purpose was to enable the smooth and efficient collection of poll tax as well as for military conscription and forced labour. At this time, the empire stretched from the foothills of the Mongolian plateau to the Yangtze River basin and would be further enlarged by forays into the northern regions of Vietnam and coastal areas close to Guangzhou. Qin commoners were conscripted to work on what would become the Great Wall. For centuries, states had built ramparts or earthen walls along their frontiers to keep out the nomads in the north as well as other warlike peoples. Between 220 and 206 BC Qin citizens worked on the Wall although little of that section remains today.

There were three unsuccessful attempts on the life of Huangdi and, indeed, he became obsessed with the avoidance of death. He eventually passed away in 210 BC during a tour of eastern China and his body was interred in a massive mausoleum that had been constructed at great expense. Although his tomb has not yet been excavated, in 1974, about half a mile from it, thousands of life-sized terracotta figures of soldiers and horses were discovered buried in three pits. The Terracotta Army, as it is known, had been put there to protect the First Emperor in death.

The Second Emperor

The First Emperor's heir, Crown Prince Fusu (died 210 BC), was not a Legalist and had opposed many of his father's measures, including the burning of texts. Prime Minister Li Si and the powerful chief palace eunuch, Zhao Gao (died 207 BC), were at odds with General Meng Tian (died 210 BC), a favourite of Fusu and feared that when Fusu took the throne they would lose power. They forged a letter, purportedly from the First Emperor, ordering Fusu and the general to commit suicide. They complied and Fusu's younger brother, 21-year-old Huhai, took the throne as Emperor Qin Er Shi (ruled 210–207 BC).

The Second Emperor became a puppet with Zhao Gao pulling the strings. The eunuch even conspired a few years later to have his old colleague, Li Si, executed. During his reign, the people's lot only got worse, hundreds of thousands sent to the frontiers to perform border protection duties while huge numbers were forced to work on public building projects. The Second Emperor was harsh in his punishment of even petty crimes and had a number of imperial princes executed or imprisoned. Meanwhile, Zhao Gao instructed the young ruler that an emperor should neither be seen nor heard. This meant that he saw no minister other than the eunuch and took advice from him alone.

In 209 BC, as a group of peasant soldiers were on their way to join the frontier garrison, they were held up by bad weather and failure to arrive on time meant death under the harsh Qin laws. Two of the officers, Cheng Shen (died 208 BC) and Wu Guang (died 208 BC), decided to rebel, becoming a focus for armed rebellions across the empire. Within a short time, the two officers had assembled an army of 10,000 men. Their uprising was doomed to failure, though, against the highly professional and organised Qin army. The struggle continued, however, under the leadership of Liu Bang (died 195 BC), a minor official of peasant origin and Xiang Yu (died 202 BC), an aristocrat. Liu Bang captured the capital Xianyang while Xiang Yu defeated the main Qin army. The Qin monarchy collapsed in 206 BC after just fifteen years, leaving the two rebel leaders to engage in a struggle for the throne that lasted several years.

Han Dynasty: 206 BC to 220 AD

Western Han: 206 BC to 9 AD

A few years earlier, Liu Bang had been a minor functionary in charge of a postal relay station. His extraordinary skills as a politician, strategist and leader led him in 206 BC to become king of Han and, in 202 BC, after victory against Xiang Yu in the Battle of Gaixia, he became emperor and founder of the Han Dynasty (ruled 202–195 BC). He assumed the name Gao – although he is more commonly known by his temple name, Gaozu – and proclaimed to his people:

'...I am come to rule over you. With you, I further agree on three laws.
For murder, death.
For injury to person, proportionate punishment.
For theft, proportionate punishment.
The remainder of the Qin laws to be abrogated.
The officials and people will continue to attend to their respective duties as heretofore. My sole object in coming here is to eradicate wrong. I desire to do violence to no one. Fear not.'

Gaozu made Chang'an his capital, a few miles from the Qin capital of Xianyang which had been burned to the ground during the rebellions. He returned to the habits of his Zhou predecessors, rewarding some of his generals with feudal estates but, on the whole, retained the machinery of the Qin's centralised government.

There was urgent work to be done to restore the fortunes of the empire and in the first fifty years of Han rule, measures were introduced to revive the economy, promote agriculture and to help those who worked the land. Gaozu encouraged soldiers to return to working on the land by freeing them from forced labour duties for periods of between six and twelve years. Population growth was also stimulated by freedom from forced labour for two years on the birth of a baby. People who had sold themselves into slavery were freed and taxes were reduced.

By the reign of the fifth and greatest Han emperor, Wu (ruled 141–87 BC), China was prospering and making bold advances in agriculture and water management. A canal-building programme was embarked upon and dams were built to limit the possibility of flooding. More land was cleared for cultivation and production of grain and many other things increased. It was a golden age. Commerce too had been increased, stimulated by the rise in production. In fact, it soon became apparent that the supply of currency would prove inadequate for the amount of buying and selling that was going on. Wealthy families, therefore, were given the right to produce their own currency. It was a tricky business, however, and prices rocketed. The emperor had to introduce a number of measures to prevent the devaluation of the currency and also created state monopolies to prevent private ones from forming. Salt and iron production were nationalised.

He put his officials in charge of all forms of transport, whether by land or sea and took back control of the production of currency. He also carried out one of the first experiments with paper money although it would be during the Tang Dynasty in the seventh century that the banknote was first issued. It was not paper that Wu used, but the hide of a rare white deer that could be found only on his estates. It was given to nobles visiting the court in exchange for 400,000 copper coins, an easy way for Wu to raise money.

The vassal states created by the first Han emperor were a threat but Wu controlled them with a law that stipulated that instead of being inherited by the oldest son, the estates were to be divided between all sons. Although Wu established an autocratic and highly centralised state, he also adopted the principles of Confucianism as his state philosophy and students of Legalist philosophy were prohibited from state appointments. Elderly scholars, who had committed them to memory many decades previously, reconstructed the Confucian classics that had been burned by the Qin. Copies of books that had been hidden at the time were brought out of their hiding places. Wu established a school to teach these classics and its students would go on to become bureaucrats in his government.

All the Han emperors had made efforts to employ the best people in important positions, and Emperor Wu was no different. He issued a proclamation asking for able men to come forward:

'Exceptional work demands exceptional men. A bolting or a kicking horse may eventually become a most valuable animal. A man who is the object of the world's detestation may live to accomplish great things. As with the intractable horse, so with the infatuated man; it is simply a question of training. We therefore command the various district officials to search for men of brilliant and exceptional talents, to be Our generals, Our ministers, and Our envoys to distant states.'

It was a principle – employing the able and promoting the worthy – that was to remain with the Chinese Empire and its bureaucracy until its end two thousand years later. It was wise because the fact that officials were appointed as a result of recommendation or, later, through the examination system, meant that they owed their position directly to the emperor, rather than through an accident of birth or inheritance. Soon, there were 30,000 students and provincial schools were also established. Examinations were introduced to test prospective officials' knowledge of the Confucian classics. The bureaucrats produced, however, were more than merely functionaries. They retained the right to criticise the government and its policies, railing against imperial extravagance, for instance. They also stood up to the powerful eunuchs, especially in the later Han period, sometimes at great risk to their careers or even their lives. Thus a balance of power was achieved between the principles of Confucianism and the bureaucracy.

The spread of learning was undoubtedly helped by the invention of paper in Han times, increasing the availability of books. This invention – the pulp papermaking process ascribed to Cai Lun (c. 50–121 AD), a Han court eunuch – brought other benefits. Paper proved an effective substitute for silk in many situations, leaving Han China with more silk to export, substantially benefiting the economy of the empire. The oldest piece of paper with writing on it was found in a Han watchtower abandoned in 110 AD in Inner Mongolia. From the Han period come not only the reconstituted classical texts but also the earliest dictionaries and the first general history of China, written by Sima Qian, the Prefect of the Grand Scribes in Han China. His masterpiece, *Records of the Grand Historian*, incorporating many first-hand accounts, covered more than two thousand years of China's history from the Yellow Emperor to Emperor Wu.

It was a remarkable period in the development of Chinese science and technology. Blast furnaces to convert iron ore into pig iron had been in operation since the late Spring and Autumn period. In Han China, a process was introduced to produce wrought iron. The most important benefit of the new iron-smelting process was the manufacture of new implements for use in agriculture. The multi-tube seed drill, for instance, invented in the second century BC, permitted farmers to plant seeds in rows instead of casting them onto the soil randomly by hand, as previously. The heavy mouldboard iron plough, which not only cut furrows but also turned the soil, was invented by the Han Chinese. Pulled by two oxen, it required only one man to control it and could sow around 11.3 acres of land in a single day.

The armillary sphere, a three-dimensional representation of the movements of the stars and planets in the celestial sphere, was invented in Han China by court astronomer Zhang Heng (78–139 AD). It used a water clock, a waterwheel and a series of gears. This extraordinary man also invented a seismometer in 132 AD that detected earthquakes from hundreds of miles away; he documented some 2,500 stars in more than 100 constellations; he wrote a new formula for *pi* and corrected mistakes in the Chinese calendar. There were many Han achievements in mathematics, possibly the greatest of which was the world's first use of negative numbers which appeared in the *Nine Chapters on the Mathematical Art*, a book composed by several generations of scholars from the tenth to the second centuries BC, its last stage being from the first century AD. It is one of the earliest surviving mathematical texts from China.

The Han also invented the rudder at the stern for steering ships, replacing the simple steering oar and allowing them to sail on the high seas. They developed the design for the junk, a vessel with a square-ended bow and stern, a flat-bottomed hull with no keel and solid transverse bulkheads. Physician Hua Tuo (c. 140–208 AD) was the first person to use anaesthesia during surgery, combining wine with a herbal concoction called *mafeisan* which translates literally as 'cannabis boil powder'. In the first century BC, Jing Fang (78–37 BC) was the first music theorist to note that 53 perfect fifths approximate 31 octaves. Like Zhang Heng, he theorised that the light of the moon was merely light reflected from the sun.

The family during the Han dynasty was patrilineal. Unlike later times, multiple generations tended not to live under one roof. Arranged marriages were customary with the father having most influence on the choice of spouse for his child. Marriage was monogamous, but those men who were wealthy enough, such as nobles and high-ranking officials, had concubines. Divorce and remarriage for both men and women was possible under certain conditions. Women were expected to obey their fathers, then their husbands and then their adult sons in old age. They were not conscripted for forced labour projects, but often took jobs – weaving, selling at market or working for one of the large textile businesses – aside from their domestic duties, to earn extra income for the family. In religion, families made sacrifices of animals and foodstuffs to gods, spirits and ancestors at temples and shrines. The emperor was the high priest of Han China, making sacrifices to

Heaven, the main deities – the Five Powers (the Three Sovereigns and Five Emperors) – and the spirits or *shen*, of mountains and rivers.

Threats From Beyond the Wall

The Middle Kingdom had been victim to countless attacks from the northern nomads since the earliest times. By the time of the Han Dynasty, a tribal confederation of the Xiongnu (Huns) had been formed that is said to have placed a quarter of a million horse-borne archers at the command of their leader. The Great Wall had failed to eradicate this menace.

Emperor Gaozu was hard-pressed by the nomads but he entered into a series of marriage alliances that became an essential part of Sino-barbarian relationships. The conciliation policy also included annual gifts of grain, silk, wine and other delicacies. This, however, did not stop the nomadic hordes from making the occasional foray into Han territory. Eventually, Emperor Wu, on his ascent to the throne, believed his armies strong enough to take on the nomads. He dispatched massive invasion forces north, capturing strongholds and, after the decisive Battle of Mobei in 119 BC, forcing the Xiongnu court to flee north of the Gobi Desert. By 111 BC, the Han had expanded into a vast territory spanning the Hexi Corridor on the northern edge of the Tibetan Plateau to Lop Nur in the northwest, establishing four new frontier commanderies in the region – Jiuquan, Zhangyi, Dunhuang and Wuwei.

Emperor Wu, who had by this time adopted Confucianism at court, had already looked to Central Asia, partly to find allies to support the Han against the Xiongnu, but also to improve the supply of horses for his army. He sent an imperial envoy, Zhang Qian (200–114 BC), west in 139 BC. Zhang was captured and held prisoner for ten years by the Xiongnu before escaping and continuing his journey to Bactria in modern Afghanistan and Ferghana in modern Uzbekistan, returning to the Han capital in 126 BC. Eleven years later, Zhang set out once more. In 101 BC, following his accounts of these distant regions, a Chinese army travelled beyond the Pamir Mountains and defeated Ferghana in battle, seizing large numbers of horses. As a result of this action, Han China gained control of valuable trade routes across Central Asia. Zhang Qian discovered that Chinese goods, including silk acquired by the Xiongnu, had made their way to the distant lands he visited, passing along the Silk Road, established in Han times, through Sogdian, Parthian, Indian and other merchants. Chinese silk was, in fact, already popular in Rome by the time of the death of Julius Caesar around 44 BC.

Meanwhile, as in Qin times, Han settlers pushed further south into more marginal upland areas, especially during the chaos of Emperor Wang Mang's rule (c. 9–23 AD). A government census in the third century established the population of China as 59 million and it is estimated from comparison of censuses that between five and ten million people migrated south during the first and early second centuries. Furthermore, the Han strengthened garrisons as far south as Vietnam.

Xin Dynasty and Later, or Eastern Han (9 AD to 220 AD)

Court official Wang Mang's seizure of the throne and short-lived Xin Dynasty (9–23 AD) briefly interrupted the Han Dynasty. He introduced a number of reforms including the well-field system of land distribution and agricultural production by which a square area of land was divided into nine identically-sized sections; the eight outer sections were privately cultivated by serfs and the central section was communally cultivated on behalf of the landowning aristocrat. The aristocrats forced him to rescind this system a few years later. He also levied a tax of 10 per cent on the wages of professionals and skilled labourers and imposed government monopolies on liquor, salt, iron, coinage, forestry and fishing.

Amidst rebellions by secret societies with names such as Red Eyebrow and Green Woodsmen, he was ousted. The weak and ineffective Han Emperor Gengshi ruled for two years, but was defeated and strangled by the rebels, one of whom, Guangwu (ruled 25–57 AD), succeeded him in what has become known as the Eastern Han Dynasty. A descendant of the Han imperial family,

Guangwu restored a strong, centralised administration and improved tax revenues. He attempted to lessen the burden of the peasant, by reducing the amount of forced labour that had to be done. Meanwhile, improved farming implements helped to increase yields.

The Han Chinese strengthened their position in Vietnam in 43 AD and it was ruled by Chinese governors. This domination lasted until 544 AD. Meanwhile, Central Asia was re-conquered and territory as far as the Caspian Sea was taken. It is astonishing to contemplate that at this point in history only Parthia (a region of modern north-eastern Iran) separated the empires of the Han Chinese and the Romans. The Chinese called the Roman Empire, 'Da Qin' (Great Qin), demonstrating their belief that it was a kind of alternative China on the other side of the world. There were only a few attempts at contact between the two empires. In 97 AD, the Chinese unsuccessfully tried to send an envoy to Rome but several Roman emissaries are recorded as having made it to China, the first being in 166 AD.

Although there was a century of comparative peace, the same old problems began to re-emerge. The power of the landowners increased and impoverished peasants bore the brunt of the large amount of tax their masters, the landowners, had to pay to the government. They became serfs once again. The Han emperor began to face a dual threat, firstly from the powerful families that had been created who had their own armies and secondly from the rebel gangs that were recruiting the dissatisfied peasants. There was another threat, however, from within the imperial court itself.

Decline and Fall of the Han

During the second century, the eunuchs who worked as palace servants became increasingly involved in court politics and violent power struggles erupted between the various relatives of the empresses and empress dowagers. In 124 the eunuchs staged a coup against Empress Dowager Yan (died 126) and crowned a 10 year-old royal child as Emperor Shun (ruled 125–144), aiming to control him. Shun reigned for nineteen years, being succeeded by his son, Chong (ruled 144–45). By 159, however, the eunuchs were in complete control and anyone who opposed them was eliminated. The ensuing chaos reduced the amount of revenue coming into the Han treasury. In 184, a Daoist religious cult, the Way of Great Peace, launched the Yellow Turban Rebellion and the Five Pecks of Rice Rebellion. When Emperor Ling (ruled 168–169) died, around 2,000 palace eunuchs were massacred, placing power in the hands of a number of aristocrats and warlords who divided the empire amongst themselves.

3. Turmoil, Re-unification and a Golden Age

Six Dynasties: Age of Disunity (220 to 589 AD)

For the next 369 years, China was torn asunder by political division and governments that were unable to control the territories over which they ruled. Between 256 and 316, the empire was briefly re-united under the Western Jin dynasty and, from 317 to 420, the Eastern Jin Dynasty existed. But after that there was a return to internal squabbling and a period ensued during which foreign rulers took over in the north while in the south a group of aristocrats ruled. These were harsh times for the peasantry as personal bondage grew and social inequality was rife. As the Confucian view of life became less regarded, people turned to religions that promised salvation and the ability to rise above the trials and tribulations of daily existence. This increased the popularity of Daoist cults as well as the newly arrived Buddhist religion which captivated China.

Three Kingdoms (220–280)

The period of the Three Kingdoms was one of the bloodiest in Chinese history. A census taken during the late Han period reported the population to be around 50 million. A later census, during the early Western Jin dynasty arrived at a population of just 16 million. The Jin dynasty census was far less comprehensive than the earlier one, but there certainly were many millions fewer in China.

The generals who had divided the empire after the fall of the Han Dynasty developed into independent warlords. In the north was the state of Wei which occupied the China plain. It lay between the states of Qin and Qi and took in parts of modern Henan, Hebei, Shanxi and Shandong. Cao Cao (155–220), the second-last chancellor of the Eastern Han Dynasty, had enjoyed huge power in the dying years of Han. A skilful poet and brilliant military genius, he established a dictatorship in northern China. When he died in 220, his son Cao Pi (187–226) succeeded him. It was Cao Pi who forced the abdication of the last Han emperor and he founded the Wei Dynasty at the former Han capital, Luoyang.

Two other claimants to the imperial throne stood in the way of Cao Pi. The brothers Sun Ce (175–200) and Sun Quan (182–252) established the state of Wu in the central and lower Yangtze valley while a distant relative of the Han imperial family, Liu Bei (161–223), established himself in Shu, in the area of modern Sichuan.

Wei, with the greatest population and largest army of the three, eventually defeated Shu and took its capital Chengdu in 263. The taste of victory was short-lived, however. Just two years later, Sima Yan, Duke of Jin (236–290), seized the throne of Wei after forcing the ruler Cao Huan (246–302) to abdicate and established the Jin Dynasty (later known as Western Jin). In March 280, after a major Jin offensive, involving naval attacks, the southern state of Wu collapsed and the capital Jianye was captured. The Jin Dynasty had succeeded in reunifying China and the bloody Three Kingdoms era was at an end.

Jin Dynasty: 265–420

Western and Eastern Jin

It had been an odd century. Against a background of warfare and death, there was an increased interest in philosophy and an explosion of self-expression in the arts, especially in poetry. Several of the major political players, such as Cao Cao and Cao Pi, were brilliant poets as well as military strategists. Around this time, the gifted but scandalous group of poets, the Seven Sages of the Bamboo Grove, were writing. One rode through the capital in a cart drawn by a deer with a servant following behind carrying a large jug of wine in case it was needed. Another followed carrying a spade so that he might be able to bury his master wherever the booze might finally put paid to him. Needless to say, conservative Confucianists were outraged by such antics.

The earliest book on the subject of alchemy was written in the second century, as a result of the fascination with elixirs and immortality and at the start of the fourth century a massive tome on the art of achieving immortality was published. It is worth pointing out that the preoccupation with elixirs of immortality contributed to the early deaths of several emperors who overdosed on toxic substances claimed to guarantee eternal life. The period has been the subject of countless romantic tales and legends, the most famous of which is the historical novel *Romance of the Three Kingdoms* written by Luo Guanzhong (c. 1330–1400) in the fourteenth century.

Meanwhile, the mandarins evolved into an effete caste who regarded even indirect contact with manual labour to be degrading. They grew their fingernails very long to prove that they never indulged in such activity. Rouged, powdered and perfumed, they cared little for the work they had been appointed to carry out, sometimes not even knowing in what capacity they were employed. One mandarin, when asked what office he held, is reported to have replied that he thought it might be master of horse, because he saw a lot of them being led about the place. Later, when the capital was under siege, the mandarins stayed put in the city that they never left and starved to death, dressed in their finest clothes.

Unfortunately, however, the Western Jin never managed to become a centralised imperial authority and the emperors faced persistent dissent from both their civil service which they never fully controlled and the families of empresses. Old habits became prevalent again, such as rewarding imperial princes with estates and appointing people because of their social rank rather than according to ability. A series of succession struggles ensued and between 291 and 305 there was outright civil war.

In 317, Sima Rui (276–323) founded the Eastern Jin Dynasty at Jiankang, the territory over which he ruled as Prince of Jin, rather than emperor, extending across much of today's southern China. It was a period during which significant numbers of Chinese migrated south from China's central plain, but the Eastern Jin rulers had little influence, military power being exercised by men who were not members of the royal family. Eventually, there was a series of revolts and the end of the Jin Dynasty arrived when the throne was seized by the great general Liu Yu. From 420 to 422, he ruled as Emperor Wu of the Liu Song Dynasty, the first of the four Southern Dynasties.

Southern and Northern Dynasties (420–589)

Much of the fifth and sixth centuries was taken up with further disunity in the period known as the Southern and Northern Dynasties. As with most of the previous two centuries, it was a time of civil war and political chaos, but was also a time during which the arts and culture flourished. Power became based on two distinct areas – the Yellow River basin northwards towards the Great Wall and the Yangtze basin and the lands south of it as far as the Red River. During a period of more than a hundred years, known as the Sixteen Kingdoms (304–439), chaos ruled in the north and it appeared that Chinese civilisation was a thing of the past. Bandits roamed the countryside and the population was ravaged by famine. Power had devolved to a local level with villages building their own fortifications against enemy forces. Money no longer circulated and the economy collapsed.

There were nomad immigrants and in the fourth century, various warlords vied for power. The Tuoba from Mongolia were the first to establish themselves properly, proclaiming their own dynasty, the Northern Wei (439–534). Opponents were eradicated and they set up their capital at Luoyang, spreading westward into Central Asia. As time passed, the Tuoba settled and became fully integrated, Chinese becoming the language of the imperial court. Others, such as the Xianbei from southern Manchuria, spread into northern Shanxi province and from there launched raids on other tribes and Chinese towns and villages.

The nomad incursions from the north forced many people to flee south, including numerous scholars and intellectuals. This influx of people and ideas resulted in benefits for the economy of southern China which had always lagged behind that of the more agriculturally successful Yellow River valley to the north. Greater agricultural know-how was applied and water control initiatives were instigated, particularly in the valley of the Yangtze. For the first time, the south became a match for the north in terms of its economy, culture and politics. The south was ruled by four dynasties during this period – the Liu Song (420–479), the Southern Qi (479–502), the Liang (502–557) and the Chen (557–589). Their rulers were, on the whole, generals who seized power, holding it for a number of decades, but failing to pass it on to their heirs.

Part of the problem was that a hereditary aristocracy had emerged at the top of the civil service that secured automatic access to the best positions for people with family connections. Many established large estates and poverty-stricken refugees from the north were engaged to work the land, although they were little more than serfs. This was undoubtedly exploitative and prejudiced but it could be said that, at a time when the state was providing no basis for the preservation of Chinese culture, these families did.

Sui Dynasty (589–618)

It made little difference to the poor who was in charge, however. They were still burdened with high rents, punitive taxation and the trials of forced labour. In the middle of the sixth century, this led to increasing numbers of rebellions by oppressed peasants and tribes of nomads. Eventually, in 581, the Northern Wei throne was seized by a member of the royal family who would become emperor as Wen (ruled 581–604) in the short-lived Sui Dynasty. Wen initiated a series of reforms designed to strengthen his empire in readiness for the achievement of his ultimate objective, the conquest of the south and the reunification of China. By 588, he had assembled a massive force of more than half a million troops along the northern bank of the Yangtze, from Sichuan to the Pacific Ocean. A year later, the southern Chen Dynasty surrendered and Wen's troops were marching into Jiangkang (modern Nanjing) bringing more than three centuries of separation to a close.

Emperor Wen succeeded in bankrupting the state treasury with his wars and construction projects, but a great deal was also achieved during his reign. As the Han emperors had done, he established granaries as sources for food that helped to control market prices. His son Yang (ruled 604–618) came to power, after, it is suspected, he had murdered his father. He ordered the building of the Grand Canal in today's Zhejiang and southern Jiangsu provinces which would become the longest canal or artificial river in the world. A road was built alongside the canal and relay post stations were added. It grew to 1,200 miles, allowing the central government to exploit the growing wealth of the Yangtze valley. It also did away with the need for armies on the march to be self-supporting. Now they could be supplied with materials brought from the south to the north on the canal.

Yang restored Confucian education and the examination system for bureaucrats. However, he also levied excessive taxes, to fund his initiatives and costly wars against Korea and he became increasingly unpopular. The peasants rebelled, forcing him to flee to Jiangdu (modern Yangzhou) where he was assassinated by an adviser. The Li family – members of the northwest military aristocracy – seized power and established the Tang dynasty.

Buddhism

Spiritually, the peasants during this period were drawn to various Daoist sects. These incorporated local superstitions and spirits. Some sects promulgated ideas of inner hygiene and nature cure, eschewing meat, grain and wine. Some even believed their own breath and saliva to represent the purest form of nourishment. However, as the world seemed to be falling apart and belief in government appeared to be misplaced, a religion suddenly appeared in China that had been taking Asia by storm. It had little in common with the rational humanistic traditions of Chinese classical thought, but Buddhism arrived in the empire at the right moment, towards the end of the turbulent third century.

The historical Buddha ('enlightened one'), Siddhartha Gautama, was a prince who lived in a northern state of India, near Nepal, about the same time as Confucius, around 500 BC. One day, while he was undergoing a spiritual crisis, he experienced a moment of enlightenment while meditating under the Bo tree – the tree of knowledge. His route to personal enlightenment pursued a path of moderation, following a middle way. The pain of existence, he taught, can only be eliminated by eradicating desires and that can only be achieved by living right and having correct thoughts. The objective is to break the cycle of rebirth and death – Buddhists believe in reincarnation – achieving Nirvana, the state of complete serenity when the spirit has merged with eternal harmony. This can only be achieved through a series of rebirths, each life better than the last. The sinner, however, will be reincarnated, for example, as a dog or a pig.

Buddhism arrived in northern China from Central Asia, although Indian traders sailing to the Middle Kingdom across the southern ocean may also have been partly responsible. There had been Buddhists at the court of Emperor Ming Ti who sat on the throne during the Later Han from 57 to 75 AD, but it was during the so-called Period of Disunity that it really took hold, offering the chance of individual salvation and freedom from the stresses of life at a time when those seemed remote.

Soon, Buddhist missionaries were visiting China, making conversions and ensuring that previous converts remained true. New followers were recruited and Buddhist texts were translated into Chinese by scholars such as An Shigao (died 168), a Parthian prince who renounced his claim to the Parthian throne to spread the Buddhist word. Kumarajiva (344–413), who was born in Central Asia but had Indian roots, was a Kuchean Buddhist monk and prolific translator of Buddhist texts from Sanskrit to Chinese. Chinese Buddhists made pilgrimages to the source of their faith in India, the most famous probably being Faxian (337-c. 422) who travelled to India – including Lumbini, birthplace of Gautama Buddha – Sri Lanka and Kapilavastu in modern Nepal between 399 and 412. He described his travels in *A Record of Buddhist Kingdoms, Being an Account by the Chinese Monk Faxian of his Travels in India and Ceylon in Search of the Buddhist Books of Discipline*.

Buddhism would continue to flourish in China until the eighth century. Great temples were carved out of cliffs and statues of the Buddha were also hewn from rock, as in the 50-feet-tall version at the Yungang Grottoes near the modern city of Datong in the province of Shanxi. These, the most ancient of such carvings, were made in the fifth and sixth centuries and stretch for a kilometre along the sandstone cliff face. During the Sui and Tang dynasties, Buddhist institutions became embedded in Chinese life. The monasteries offered schooling for local children and they also provided lodgings for travellers. They amassed huge estates worked by large numbers of peasants and established businesses such as oil presses and mills. They even lent money or provided a pawnbroking service, contributing hugely to local economies. The romances and tales that were told in Tang times were mostly of Buddhist origin and Chinese Buddhist schools were well established, such as the Pure Land or the Chan school (Zen in Japan). The Chan school venerated a series of patriarchs, the first of whom was Bodhidharma, a monk who had come to China from India in the early sixth century.

Towards the end of the Tang dynasty, however, there was growing antipathy to Buddhism, partly because it was still perceived as foreign and partly because it was seen as an economic drain on the country, particularly as the court's finances diminished. In 841 the emperor launched a campaign of suppression of Buddhism and other foreign religions. Buddhism, already threatened by the spread of Islam, lost a great deal of its momentum in China. Many monasteries and chapels were destroyed and many Chinese Buddhist schools of thought did not survive.

Advances in the Midst of Turmoil

Despite the devastating turmoil and chaos of this period, there were many exciting advances. Chinese government official and mechanical engineer, Ma Jun (c. 220-c. 265), invented a directional compass, the South Pointing Chariot that was operated not by magnetism, but by differential gears. One of the most brilliant minds of his day, he also invented an improved silk loom that worked five times faster than previous looms and a wheel to raise water to be used in irrigation. Mathematician Zu Chongzhi (429–500), was the first person to establish the value of the mathematical constant *pi* (π) – the ratio of a circle's circumference to its diameter – to eight decimal places. His best estimation of the value would hold for 900 years. A geography of the waterways of China was produced during this time as well as an important encyclopedia. The wheelbarrow did not come into use in Europe until sometime between 1170 and 1250, but the Chinese were using one-wheeled carts from the second century and the first recorded mention of one was in 30 BC.

Tang Dynasty (618 to 907)

The reunified empire enjoyed strong economic growth under its next imperial dynasty, the Tang. This was aided by the construction of the Grand Canal linking the north and south of the empire as well as the expansion of trade both within China and internationally. Chang'an, the Tang capital, with a population of around a million, became the largest and most cosmopolitan city in the world. Until the An Lushan Rebellion that occurred between 755 and 763, the Chinese were open to cultures from around the world, happy to absorb influences in music, art and fashion and even in their Buddhist religion.

Li Yuan, the Duke of Tang, governor of the modern day province of Shanxi, rebelled with his son against his cousin, the Sui ruler Emperor Yang (ruled 604–618). They were accompanied in the rebellion by the duke's equally militant daughter Princess Pingyang (598–623) who rode at the head of her own force. On 18 June 618, while he was occupying Chang'an, Li Yuan declared himself Emperor Gaozu (ruled 618–626), the first emperor of a new dynasty, the Tang. Eight years later, he was forcibly deposed by his son, Li Shimin, Prince of Qi, who reigned as Taizong (ruled 626–49).

Emperor Taizong had been ruthless in his pursuit of power, having killed his two brothers and their ten sons before forcing his father to abdicate in his favour. Nonetheless, his reign proved very successful.

The early Tang rulers restored and applied more effectively the equal field system of land ownership and distribution that had been in use since the Six Dynasties. It worked on the basis that the government owned all land and would assign it to individual families. Everyone, including slaves, had an entitlement of land that was governed by their ability to provide labour. When the owners died, the land reverted to the state and was reassigned. It was a system designed to ensure that every piece of land was used, that everyone had an opportunity to earn a livelihood and to prevent the establishment of large estates by powerful families. It also enabled the government to raise taxes more efficiently. Thus, the peasantry was kept solvent and free, rendering it unnecessary for them to sell themselves into slavery or serfdom. Or to consider rebellion.

The first Sui emperor had reintroduced the Han system of examinations based on the Confucian classics for prospective bureaucrats and the Tang emperors expanded the system. Some examinations included questions on the entire field of literature in which candidates had to compose poems and write essays, as well as write about political and administrative problems. They sat exams in regional centres, the successful ones then being summoned to the capital where they sat another series of examinations, both written and oral. In this way, the Tang ensured they had officials capable of governing their immense empire and the system remained in place until the twentieth century. It was worth the hard work it took to become a state official for they were exempt, very often, from taxation, forced labour and military service. They could enrich themselves and provide privileges for members of their families.

Supreme power was wielded, of course, by the emperor, advised by a small council of ministers. The empire was divided into prefectures which were subdivided into districts, each governed by an official. The Tang used the 'three chiefs system' to collect taxes, a collaborative system in which each had responsibility for the others around them. In this system, groups of people shared mutual responsibility for each others' behaviour and for each others' payment of their tax. Five families made up a neighbourhood, five neighbourhoods constituted a village and five villages an association, each level of the system having its own chief.

The Tang built on the code of law that had been introduced by the Sui. The earliest code to survive contains 500 articles detailing the punishments for a long list of crimes. These ranged from light beatings – ten blows with a light stick, to heavier beatings – a hundred blows with a weightier stick that often proved fatal. Exile, penal servitude and execution also featured. The legal principles enshrined in the Tang code of law could be found in those of every dynasty that followed.

The state controlled a great deal of the economy in Tang times. Mining had been state-controlled for a considerable time, in particular mining for copper and silver which were needed for the minting of coins and for the manufacture of weapons and tools. The state employed large numbers of workers and such work earned exemption from forced labour or military duties. Other nationalised industries included salt production and transport. Contracts were required for the purchase of slaves, horses, oxen, land and houses, tax being levied on every purchase. Silk production expanded during the Tang dynasty, many looms working on the relentless production of silk to be presented as tribute at the imperial court. There was also an increase in the production of porcelain. Merchants, were, however, still looked down on by officials and the population at large. They also paid most taxes.

In the seventh century, the imperial court was dominated by Empress Wu Zetian (ruled 690–705), the only woman in Chinese history to assume the title of Empress Regnant. She had arrived at the court as a concubine of Emperor Gaozong (ruled 649–83) but within a few years the emperor had ousted his empress and installed Wu in her place. Once installed, she began the process of eliminating all her opponents and, when her husband suffered a stroke in 660, she took full control. He died in 683 but Wu held onto power. She is believed by some to have killed her oldest son, Li Hong (652–75), and later had another son, Crown Prince Li Xian (653–84) exiled. She deposed yet another son, and installed her youngest son, Ruizong (ruled 684–90, 710–12) as puppet emperor. In 690, she declared herself emperor of a new dynasty, the Zhou. Aged 80 and ailing, Empress Wu was finally overthrown in a coup in 705 that returned her son Zhongzong (ruled 684, 705–10) to power and she died the following year. Some have seen her as an evil usurper of the Chinese throne, but there can be little doubt of her determination and political savvy.

After Zhongzong was poisoned by his wife, the throne passed to his son, Emperor Shang Di (ruled 710). Following his brief rule, Ruizong returned to the dragon throne but, in 712, believing that astrological indications signalled the need for a change of ruler, he abdicated in favour of his nephew who became Emperor Xuanzong (ruled 712–56).

Emperor Xuanzong, Yang Guifei and the End of the Tang Dynasty

It was during the reign of Xuanzong that Tang culture reached its zenith. The court of his grandmother, Empress Wu, had certainly championed high culture but Xuanzong took it to new heights. He staged magnificent state ceremonies and codified state ritual. He invited Daoist and Buddhist scholars to his court, including those of the new Tantric school of Buddhism. He founded a new academy for poetry and enjoyed music. The great horse painter, Han Gan (706–83), served at his court. Han was reputed to be able not only to render the physical features of a horse in his beautiful paintings, but also its spirit.

Xuanzong was no less attentive to more mundane administrative matters, however. He reformed the equal-field system and to safeguard his tax revenues ordered a new census. To guard against the threats posed by Turks, Uighurs and Tibetans along China's borders, he established a ring of military provinces along the frontier.

Sources tell of tens of thousands of beautiful young women

being forced to live in Xuanzong's palace as concubines – many more than other Tang emperors. In the emperor's eyes, however, one stood out. Yang Guifei (719–56) had become imperial consort to Xuanzong following the death of Consort Wu in 737. Princess Yang was entertained by the company of one of the emperor's military governors, An Lushan (c. 703–57). To please Yang, the ruler showered An Lushan with favours and allowed him to amass large numbers of troops along the northern borders. In 755, however, An Lushan rebelled and marched on Luoyang and Chang'an. Xuanzong fled west but his troops mutinied and told him that he must have Princess Yang killed. She was strangled but the aging emperor was so distressed that he abdicated in favour of his son who became Emperor Suzong (ruled 756–62). His abdication brought to an end one of the most brilliant periods of Chinese court culture.

An Lushan was assassinated but soon other rebel leaders were emerging to carry on his fight. There was war in the provinces for the next decade and by 763, the Chinese Empire was once again in a parlous state, with taxes not being sent to the government and peasants, consequently, bearing an even heavier tax burden. Once again landlords began to amass large tracts of land. A wave of peasant uprisings in the 870s were defeated but the regional military governors (*jiedushi*) who had united to defeat the peasants had been granted increased powers and by the early years of the tenth century, they were no longer subject to the authority of the imperial government. Eventually in 904, Emperor Zhaozong (ruled 880–900, 901-04) was assassinated. His son briefly occupied the throne but was forced to yield power to former military governor Zhu Quanzhong who was serving as a general for the state of Qi and ruled the Later Liang Dynasty as Emperor Taizu (ruled 907–10). Once again, the north and the south of the empire were divided.

4. Chaos, Appeasement and Invasion

Five Dynasties and Ten Kingdoms (907 to 960)

The years from 907 to 960 brought more political upheaval to China. During these fifty-three years, five dynasties rose and fell in the north and more than a dozen independent states were established, mainly in the south of the empire, although only ten of these are usually listed.

The first northern dynasty was the Later Liang (907–23), founded by Zhu Quanzhong (852–912) who came to be known as Emperor Taizu. He controlled much of central China and, putting all his efforts into unifying the north, he was unable to make advances in the south. He was murdered by his son, Zhu Yougui (c. 888–913), Prince of Ying, who ruled only for a few months before being deposed by a rebellion led by his brother Zhu Youzhen who ruled until 923 and is sometimes known as Emperor Mo. His death marked the end of the longest of the Five Dynasties. The succeeding dynasty, the Later Tang, was the first of three dynasties ruled by the Turkic tribe, the Shatuo. Lasting for just thirteen years, it controlled much of northern China.

The Later Liang Dynasty had been engaged in constant battle with the State of Jin which was situated in modern-day Shanxi. Jin expanded under the leadership of firstly Li Keyong (856–908) and then his son, Li Cunxu (885–926). After Li Cunxu succeeded in overthrowing the Later Liang with the help of the nomadic Khitan from the northern steppe, he moved the capital back to the old Tang capital in the east, Luoyang, founding the Later Tang Dynasty (923–936) which he referred to as 'Restored Tang'. He died in an officers' rebellion after being on the throne for only three years.

Relations with the Khitan had soured by this time and the situation remained unstable for the remaining ten years of the dynasty.

In 936, Shi Jingtang (ruled 936–42) son-in-law of a previous emperor, Li Siyuan (ruled 926–33), seized the capital with the help of the Khitan and established his own dynasty, the Later Jin. Seven years later, the Khitan declared war on the Later Jin, capturing the capital Kaifeng. The Khitan now controlled large swathes of China, but, unwilling to control them, withdrew from them early the following year. Power was seized by the military governor, Liu Zhiyuan, in 947. A third successive Shatuo dynasty was established and named the Later Han dynasty. However, it was the shortest-lived of the Five Dynasties. A coup in 951 deposed Liu's son Chengyou (ruled 948–51) and put General Guo Wei (904–54), a Han Chinese, on the throne as first ruler of the Later Zhou dynasty, ruling as Emperor Taizu. His successor, Chai Rong (ruled 954–60), ruled as Emperor Shizong. Some gains in the south plus his early death at thirty-eight, leaving a six-year-old heir, helped ease the path to the eventual reunification of China under the Song Dynasty.

In southern China, meanwhile, the Ten Kingdoms ran generally concurrently, each consisting of a specific area of the region. Former Tang military governor, Yang Xingmi (ruled 902-05), founded the Kingdom of Wu that existed from 902 until 937 in the area of the modern Chinese provinces of Jiangsu, Anhui and Jianxi in south-central China. A coup by Li Bian (ruled 937–43), founder of the Southern Tang kingdom, ended the Kingdom of Wu. Emperor Yuanzong (ruled 943–61) expanded the state's territory, taking in Min, Yin and Chu. In 961, however, he submitted to the growing power of the Song Dynasty and in 975 his state was invaded and formally subsumed by the Song.

The longest-lasting and one of the most powerful of the Ten Kingdoms was Wuyue, founded by Qian Liu (ruled 907–32) after the fall of the Tang Dynasty in 907. It covered an area taking in modern Zheijiang province as well as parts of modern southern Jiangzu province on China's east coast. Famous for its learning and culture, it eventually surrendered to the Song Dynasty in 978. The Kingdom of Min was founded in 909 by Wang Shenzhi (ruled 909–25) who took the title Prince of Min. It was conquered by the Southern Tang in 945. Situated along China's southern coast, with its capital at modern-day Guangzhou, the Kingdom of Southern Han was declared by Liu Yan (ruled 917–42) in 917, initially as Great Yue. He changed the name the following year, declaring that, as his surname Liu was the same as the surname of the Han emperors, he must be a descendant of that eminent dynasty. Southern Han submitted to Song Dynasty rule in 971.

Former military governor Ma Yin (ruled 907–30) founded the Kingdom of Chu, establishing his capital at modern Changsha. The kingdom, consisting of the areas of Hunan and modern northeastern Guangxi, was absorbed by the Southern Tang in 951. The state of Former Shu, consisting of most of present-day Sichuan, western Hubei and parts of southern Gansu and Shaanxi, was established by Wang Jian (ruled 907–18) after the fall of the Tang Dynasty. An ineffective heir led to the surrender of the state to the Later Tang Dynasty in 965.

Although things were not quite so bad as in northern China during this period, the south was still torn asunder by conflict. Wu and later Southern Tang were engaged in persistent quarrels with their neighbours. Although the most powerful of the southern kingdoms for some time, Southern Tang was unable to resist the incursions of the Later Zhou Dynasty in the late 950s, ceding to it all of its land north of the Yangtze. Soon, however, a new force arrived on the scene, determined to re-unify the empire, north and south.

Song Dynasty (960 to 1279)

Northern Song (960 to 1126)

The brilliant Later Zhou military commander, Zhao Kuangyin, had the throne thrust upon him in 960 by his troops. The last Later Zhou emperor, Shizong, had been succeeded by his infant son and the army feared that the Dowager Empress would seize control. Zhao was, therefore, presented to his troops as Emperor Taizu (ruled

960–76) and soon after entered the capital city. He adroitly invited all his generals to resign, providing them with ample pensions that would enable them to live well, thus removing any danger of future military coups and ensuring that the army was entirely under his control. Desirous of unity and peace, the remaining southern states submitted to his rule and within twenty years two centuries of warfare and political chaos were over and the Middle Kingdom was one again.

The Song emperors were descended from a family of officials in the area of modern Beijing. Their dynasty consisted of five unusually competent and enlightened rulers whose lengthy reigns brought stability and prosperity to China. After centuries of turmoil and bloodshed, the Song Dynasty ushered in a period of artistic and technical excellence that surpassed any yet experienced. China under the Song came closer to the Confucian ideal of the state than at any other period.

Taizu established a strong central government, re-introducing the examination system in order to find the most able officials. Examinations were held every three years at district level and, of the thousands who entered, two hundred were annually appointed during the Song Dynasty. The exams were now a physical test as much as an intellectual one, candidates having to remain in cubicles for several days and nights, eating only food they had brought with them. In order to prevent fraudulent results, the exams were taken anonymously. Although colleges were opened in the provinces in the eleventh century, all education beyond elementary was aimed at getting candidates through the official examinations. A National University was established at Kaifeng to further help prospective candidates. Nepotism still allowed the scions of great families to make their way to the top, however, and positions could also, on occasion, be purchased. In spite of efforts to broaden the selection process, around fifty per cent of new recruits came from a family with a bureaucratic tradition.

The focus on the bureaucracy brought with it some disadvantages, however, and the Song Dynasty is noted for the vast amount of bureaucratic documentation that it produced. For instance, rules concerning the reception of Korean envoys amounted to 1,500 volumes.

The northeastern provinces of China were still ruled by Khitan nomads who posed a constant threat to the empire. They controlled a vast expanse of territory that also included land north of the Wall as well as Manchuria. The Song twice launched attacks to recover the sixteen provinces that had been ceded to the Khitan by a northern ruler but on both occasions they were driven back. In 1004, when the Khitan attacked, the emperor pacified them by accepting the status quo and paying them a substantial annual tribute. Meanwhile, the Xia nomads who controlled the Kansu corridor in the northwest that included the route to central Asia and the Old Silk Road also launched damaging attacks on Song territories. Once again the Song agreed to pay a punishing indemnity to their enemy, a decision that stirred up huge debate in the empire.

This subjugation of the military to civil interests by appeasement of an encroaching enemy and the low opinion of most people for soldiers was typical of the Song Dynasty. However, the Song army more than tripled in size between 979 and 1041, amounting to around 1,250,000 men. Armaments were produced in prodigious quantities and it is estimated that spending on the military ate up around seventy-five per cent of the empire's revenue. It was during the Song Dynasty that gunpowder was invented. The Chinese already had explosives. They used bamboo crackers to frighten away evil spirits and in the tenth century they were attaching incendiary projectiles to arrows. Grenades that produced smoke, firework rockets and mines were being used in the eleventh century. The first formula for gunpowder made from coal, saltpetre and sulphur was created in 1044 and later in the period it was discovered that gunpowder could also be used as a propellant, allowing troops to create mortars with firing tubes made of iron or bronze.

Despite the fragmentation of the empire between 750 and 1100, the population of China doubled, from approximately 50 million to 100 million by the latter date. This population explosion was the result of an increase in food production, especially the expansion of rice cultivation in both the north and the south. Commerce expanded, peasants were able to use their surplus production to buy luxuries such as tea, oil and wine and they sold products such as these through brokers. Specialisation was practised by some farmers and in Fujian, Sichuan and Guangdong, farmers turned their land over to the cultivation of sugar cane. Transport to move these goods around the country became important and the inland and coastal shipping industries received a boost, as did, of course, shipbuilding.

Foreign trade was encouraged and officials were sent abroad to persuade traders to come and buy Chinese goods. Chinese traders also sailed the East China Sea, the Yellow Sea, the Indian Ocean, and the Red Sea, aided by the development of larger ships, powered both by sail and by oar. The adaptation of the compass for navigational use was the primary factor in this maritime development. The ancient Chinese had discovered that lodestone – naturally magnetised ore or iron – suspended and allowed to spin freely, would always turn in the direction of the magnetic poles. They began to use early compasses for geomancy – the search for gems and the most favourable positioning of houses. On ships it usually took the form of a magnetised needle floating in a bowl of water, although the dry compass is also thought to have been used.

Since the seventh century, the Chinese had used the technique of wood block printing to produce full-page texts and pictures. Printing by movable type was invented by Bi Sheng (990–1051) sometime between 1041 and 1048. His remarkable technique is described by Chinese scholar and official Shen Kuo (1031–1095) in his *Writings Beside the Meng Creek*:

'During the reign of Chingli, [1041–1048] Bi Sheng, a man of unofficial position, made movable type. His method was as follows: he took sticky clay and cut in it characters as thin as the edge of a coin. Each character formed, as it were, a single type. He baked them in the fire to make them hard. He had previously prepared an iron plate and he had covered his plate with a mixture of pine resin, wax, and paper ashes. When he wished to print, he took an iron frame and set it on the iron plate. In this he placed the types, set close together. When the frame was full, the whole made one solid block of type. He then placed it near the fire to warm it. When the paste [at the back] was slightly melted, he took a smooth board and pressed it over the surface, so that the block of type became as even as a whetstone. For each character there were several types, and for certain common characters there were twenty or more types each, in order to be prepared for the repetition of characters on the same page. When the characters were not in use he had them arranged with paper labels, one label for each rhyme-group, and kept them in wooden cases.'

Production of silk, lacquer and ceramics attained technical perfection during the Song Dynasty. There were small family-based silk producers as well as government workshops. Workshops also produced exquisite ceramics, some areas acquiring reputations for the production of superior goods. Paper-makers benefitted from the increased demand for books, documents, money and wrapping paper. There were considerable advances in metallurgy, leading to an increase in iron production. The initial need for charcoal had deforested parts of northern China, but bituminous coke had replaced it by the end of the eleventh century. Hydraulic machinery used to drive bellows and the use of explosives to excavate mines also contributed to the expansion in iron production.

The growth of the economy led to a change in emphasis from the countryside to the town and the rapid growth of China's cities. Houses were made of several storeys and led straight out onto the streets rather than being built behind walls. Kaifeng, the Song capital until 1126, was as large as the Tang capital, Chang'an. Meanwhile, there were numerous provincial cities with populations of 50,000 or more.

Southern Song (1127 to 1279)
The Jurchens were a Turkic people from eastern Manchuria who rebelled against the Khitans' Liao state in 1115 and proclaimed the

Jin Dynasty. Initially, the Song allied with them against the Khitans but, after a few years, this alliance crumbled and in 1126, in what is known as the Jingkang Incident, the Jurchens captured Kaifeng after a two-month siege. The Emperor Huizong (ruled 1101–25), a talented painter and calligrapher and one of the most cultured of all Chinese emperors, had abdicated in favour of his son Emperor Qinzong (ruled 1126–27) but both were captured and taken to the northeast with all the other members of the imperial family. Negotiations were undertaken, but Huizong died in captivity in 1135.

Meanwhile, those who had managed to flee to the south installed another son of Huizong, Gaozong (ruled 1127–62), as emperor. By 1138, the Song court was established at Hangzhou and most of the region south of the Huai River was under its control. This period following the loss of the north of the empire is known as the Southern Song. Efforts were, of course, made to re-take the north, most notable among them being that of Yue Fei (1103–42), a general who defeated one Jin Dynasty force after another and set up camp within range of Kaifeng before he was recalled to the south by the emperor and executed. Emperor Gaozong feared that if Yue continued to be successful, the Jurchens might release the former Emperor Quinzong, and thus threaten his own rule.

The Southern Song expanded its already strong economy and developed a successful maritime trade, both oceanic and coastal. Large ports such as Guangzhou (formerly Canton), Hangzhou and Quanzhou were centres through which Chinese exports such as silks and porcelain passed en route for the Middle East and then onward to Europe. Texts, paintings and other works of art were exported to Japan and Korea, two countries that borrowed a great deal culturally from China. Coming in the other direction from Asia were luxury articles like gems, spices, ivory, cotton textiles and fine woods. Trading communities of Koreans, Persians and Arabs began to form in those ports and eastern China's coastal areas replaced the northwest corridor to Central Asia as China's gateway to the outside world.

In order to protect its lucrative maritime trade, China's first permanent navy was established in 1132. Boasting fast paddlewheel-driven vessels – worked on a treadmill principle – armed with trebuchet catapults that launched gunpowder bombs, it twice defeated massive Jin armadas. Funding such projects, however, was not without controversy as the government seized land in private ownership in order to raise revenue. This antagonised the upper echelons of Song society.

The loss of the north helped to stimulate the economy of the south. The transportation of goods to the capital had always constituted a large percentage of Chinese trade and having the capital at Hangzhou in the south made such transportation of goods more cost-effective, using the numerous streams and canals of the region. There was even a lucrative trade in rice, tea, sugar and books with the Jin to the north. The Southern Song, meanwhile, imported horses for their cavalry from the north. Government revenue from commercial sources began to outstrip the traditional source – agriculture. At the same time, government monopolies of such items as tea, salt and wine brought in still more funds to the imperial coffers.

By 997, the late Tang government was minting 800 million coins a year and six billion were being produced by 1085. It was this hugely increased demand for currency that led to the introduction of paper money. It began with the issuing of certificates of deposit by a small group of shops with the authority of the government. In the 1120s, the world's first government-issued paper money was produced when the Southern Song government took over the system. The notes, subject to a three per cent service charge, were valid for three years, a necessity caused by the deterioration of paper. By the second half of the following century, notes circulated by the government were legal tender throughout the empire.

Hangzhou, the Southern Song capital, had been no larger than any other provincial centre when the imperial court arrived. Soon, it had grown larger, both in terms of population and economy, than Kaifeng, the former capital in the north. Traditional Chinese single-storey houses were replaced by multi-storey buildings. The bureaucratic elite lived on the Hill of Ten Thousand Pines, rich merchants living on Mount Phoenix to the south. The three-mile long Imperial Way was sixty metres wide and was partitioned along its length in order to provide a reserved passage for the emperor. Hangzhou was full of canals and reminded merchant traveller, Marco Polo (1254–1324), of his hometown, Venice. The canals were busy with barges carrying a variety of goods, the boatmen and their families living on board. There were regular traffic jams in the congested city streets as carriages, carts and porters tried to squeeze through the narrow gateways to the city or to cross the equally narrow bridges. Meanwhile, alleyways seethed with people and bustling activity. There were several markets, including a pig market in the centre of town to satisfy the hunger of the populace for pork which was followed by rice and salted fish in popularity.

Rice is believed to have first been cultivated in China about 12,000 years ago but it did not become a staple of the Chinese diet until Song times. Southern China possessed the temperature and the rainfall required for wet-field rice but hilly and marshy terrain in the south provided an obstacle to its production. The Song developed new seed strains that allowed them to grow rice in places that had previously been considered unsuitable. Furthermore, improved damming techniques and the introduction of water pumps permitted them to reclaim land at the edge of lakes, marshes and the sea. Tax incentives by the government encouraged the terracing of hillsides on which rice could be cultivated.

The wealthy elite of Hangzhou lived lives of great luxury and indulgence. They relaxed at one of the many tea-houses and enjoyed the assistance of numerous, low-paid servants. They did not even expect to have to cut up their food. It was served cut up small enough to be picked up by chopsticks. Alongside such opulence, however, was poverty on a grand scale. The birth of a child could be a disaster for a poor family and a bucket of water was often provided at birth in which to drown the newborn, a practice known euphemistically as 'bathing the baby'. Newborn babies were also abandoned in the countryside – although this was prohibited by a twelfth-century edict – or sold to the well-to-do to be brought up as servants. A foundling hospital was established from where families wanting babies could obtain them. Measures were taken to provide some relief to the poor, including the revival of state granaries and special funds. Homes were built for the elderly and pauper funerals were provided. Those poverty-stricken men who were fit and healthy were conscripted into the army.

Similar economic, commercial and social developments were occurring at the same time in Europe. Whereas such changes led there to the rise of a bourgeoisie, capitalism and, eventually, the industrial revolution, such developments failed to materialise in China, mainly because of the state control of vital elements of the economy and commerce and the power of the bureaucracy.

Painting was one of the glories of this time and an Academy of Painting was established in Hangzhou's Lingyin Temple. Some of the period's greatest painters worked there, including landscape painters, Ma Yuan (c. 1160–1225), considered the finest painter of the time, and Xia Gui (c. 1195–1224). Books were produced in great numbers. Works on pharmaceutics and acupuncture were published and twelve eminent medical experts were commissioned by the emperor to compile an encyclopedia of medicine.

The Song Dynasty was the world's most advanced society in the eleventh, twelfth and thirteenth centuries in terms of agricultural production, technology, commerce, urbanisation and living standards. It was unique in that both the cities and the countryside were controlled by officials of the government. Of course, other Asian societies had cities like those that had developed in China, but what set China apart was the scholar-official elite of the Song and later dynasties. It was not military, unlike such elites in other societies, was not hereditary and was not religious. It was devoted to duty and service and it was accessible to all who passed the required exams.

Like all China's previous dynasties, however, the Song eventually went into decline and towards the end of the thirteenth century, this age of splendour was drawing to an end in much the same way as previous ones had done. There was increasing corruption at court as well as amongst the elite and there was growing dissatisfaction amongst the peasants. Moreover, although the Song had been able to hold back the Jin, it found itself in no condition to repel the new threat that was beginning to emerge over the steppe to the north of the Jin frontiers.

5. Recovery and the End of Empire

Yuan or Mongol Dynasty (1271 to 1368)

The Rise of the Mongols

The conquest of China proper by Inner Asian tribal peoples had been going on for four centuries. The Khitans' Liao Dynasty ruled over modern-day Mongolia and parts of Kazakhstan and the Russian Far East but, as well as extracting tribute from China's emperors, it also occupied a strip of land along the northern edge of the Middle Kingdom. The Liao were defeated by the Jurchens who founded the Jin Dynasty and expanded the territory of the Liao to incorporate all of northern China. The next invader, the Mongols, had sufficient forces to conquer all of China and re-unify it once again.

The Huns had been replaced north of the Great Wall by a number of nomadic tribes, the Turks and the Tartars amongst them. For centuries, there was conflict amongst these peoples but, by the late twelfth century, a drop in temperature on the steppe had engendered a crisis. The temperature change meant that there was insufficient grass for the tribes' animals to graze. The situation was saved by one man who unified the warring tribes and led them south to the agricultural riches of China. His name was Genghis Khan (c. 1162–1227).

Genghis was the great-grandson of Khabul Khan who had defeated the Jin Dynasty on a number of occasions. He developed into not only a great and ruthless warrior who claimed that there was no greater joy than to massacre one's enemies, steal their horses and cattle and rape their women, but he also became a skilful politician. In 1206 he was appointed Great Khan, reorganising Mongol society, casting aside traditional tribal ties and creating an army based on a basic unit of 1,000 horsemen. He appointed commanders who were resolutely loyal to him and made their posts hereditary, although he could remove any of them from his position at any time. He stabilised his nation by introducing simple, but authoritarian, laws. Although illiterate himself, he ordered that the Uighur script be used for committing Mongol to writing, acknowledging the importance of written records. Following these achievements, he was now ready for one of the greatest campaigns of conquest the world has ever seen.

In the next few years Genghis defeated his tribal rivals north of the Wall before he turned his attention to defeating the Western Xia Dynasty in 1209. The Western Xia ruled over a vast amount of territory in what are now the northwestern Chinese provinces of Ningxia, Gansu, eastern Qinghai, northern Shaanxi, northeastern Xinjiang, southwest Inner Mongolia, and southernmost Outer Mongolia. Between 1212 and 1213, his armies swept across northern China, laying waste to more than ninety cities. In 1215, the Mongol army took the Jin capital Yanjing (modern-day Beijing), forcing Emperor Xuanzong to flee south to Kaifeng, leaving the Mongols to occupy the northern half of his kingdom. His next conquest was of the Western Liao which was all that remained of the Liao Dynasty.

Genghis saw the benefits of opening up trade with the Khwarezmian Empire in modern-day Iran and he sent a 500-man caravan out on the Silk Road to make its way to the empire. It was attacked, however, by the governor of the Khwarezmian city of Otrar, infuriating the Mongol leader. Envoys he sent after this incident were beheaded, forcing Genghis to take revenge. The Shah's army was defeated by a massive Mongol force and Genghis followed up by taking Samarkand and Bukhara, razing to the ground not only royal palaces but also entire towns and massacring their inhabitants. In 1220, the Khwarezmian Empire was destroyed.

The Mongols split into two separate forces. Genghis returned to Mongolia with one half of his army, raiding through Afghanistan and India, while generals Jebe and Subutai led the other half through the Caucasus and into Russia. They wintered beside the Black Sea before turning for home. Transoxiana – the portion of Central Asia that corresponds approximately with modern-day Uzbekistan, Tajikistan, southern Kyrgyzstan and southwest Kazakhstan – and Persia were now part of the Mongol Empire.

In the mid 1220s, the Tanguts of Western Xia and the defeated Jin Dynasty joined forces against what they believed to be an exhausted Mongol army. In 1226, Genghis attacked and quickly took Heisi, Ganzhou and Suzhou. Xiliang-fu fell in the autumn. A year later, he destroyed the Tangut capital, Ning Hia, and continued with his advance. Soon, he had taken the Tangut imperial family prisoner and executed them. Around this time, some sources say, Genghis Khan was castrated with a knife by a Tangut princess in revenge for his treatment of her people and to try to prevent him from raping her. He is said to have died as a result of his wounds.

As was customary, Genghis's empire was divided amongst his four sons, creating four great Mongol kingdoms – in Persia, Central Asia, southern Russia (known as the Golden Horde) and in China. Ögedei (c. 1186–1241), the third son of Genghis Khan, was proclaimed Great Khan, establishing the nomadic Mongols' first residential capital at Karakorum. To the west, meanwhile, the Mongol hordes swept into the lush grasslands of eastern Europe, seizing Hungary in 1244. A retreat was ordered by their leader Batu (1207–55), a grandson of Genghis, when it was learned that the Great Khan, Ögedei, had died.

Under Ögedei, advances in China had continued. The Mongols defeated the Xia and in 1233 linked up with the Southern Song to attack what was left of the Jin Dynasty. Shortly after, the Jin Dynasty that had occupied northern China for more than a century had been extinguished. The Mongols now controlled the whole of northern China and began to cast hungry glances to the south. Attacks began on the region of Sichuan, and the important city of Xiangyang, the gateway to the Yangtze plain, surrendered in 1236. Song generals, meanwhile, resisted Mongol advances to the east. Xiangyang was re-captured in 1239 and the only permanent gain was Chengdu, captured by the Mongols in 1241. In 1242, they took Hanzhou and invaded Sichuan but the Song ruler sued for peace and the Mongols withdrew after accepting his terms.

Following the election of Möngke (1209–59) as Great Khan in 1251, Mongol attacks on Song China increased and intensified, led by Möngke's brother Kublai (1215–94). In 1257, Möngke set out for South China, entering Sichuan the following year. He died in 1259 and Kublai succeeded him as fifth Great Khan. Kublai Khan declared himself emperor, although the Song Dynasty was still in place in southern China. He had adopted many Chinese customs and had been taught by Chinese tutors since childhood. Furthermore, he had governed a prefecture in Hebei in northeast China. As was the Chinese tradition, he declared a title for the era, calling it 'Zhong-tong' and began the construction of a new capital close to the erstwhile Jin Dynasty capital, Zhongdu, modern-day Beijing, known by that time as Dadu. In 1271, he adopted the Chinese name, Yuan, for his dynasty and decreed that the rituals enacted at his court would be Chinese.

The new emperor renewed his assault on the Southern Song, besieging for five years the city of Xiangyang which was the key to land and water travel along the Yangtze. He engaged experts in naval and siege warfare from many countries in order to prevail. At the time, the Chinese Emperor Bing (ruled 1278–79) was a mere child and, although there were many able and loyal officials and generals, there was a great deal of confusion and argument about the best way to oppose the advancing Mongols. After Kublai Khan's army crossed the Yangtze, the Empress Dowager Xie (1210–83) appealed to the Song people to rise up against the enemy and soon an army of 200,000 subjects had been assembled. The Mongols were ruthless, however, and in their march south slaughtered the entire populace of the city of Changzhou. The Empress Dowager realised that, in the face of such a force, opposition would be pointless and, to spare the people of the empire, she surrendered. In 1279, the last of the Song rulers died in a naval battle off the coast of Guangdong.

For the first time, southern China was in the hands of a people from the steppe to the north of the Wall, but at least the empire was once more united. The Mongols, however, retained their own customs and traditions, speaking their own language at court and summering in Mongolia. Some even erected tents in the grounds of Beijing palaces and lived in them. They remained bloodthirsty and competitive throughout the dynasty which was a period of assassinations, coups and fratricide.

Life under the Mongols

Kublai Khan realised quickly the necessity of winning Chinese acceptance of Mongol rule. China, after all, was not like other territories conquered by the nomads. It was a sophisticated, highly developed civilisation that had a strong sense of its own identity. The Mongols, of course, could maintain power by force of arms, but there were not enough of them and they were not culturally equipped to govern such a sophisticated society without the help of the people themselves. Kublai's solution was, therefore, to allow them to rule themselves, in effect, and the basic institutions remained unaltered.

Not much changed culturally for the Chinese under Mongol rule. The elite carried on with their cultural pursuits. Confucian temples were safeguarded and the ancient Confucian rites and ceremonies continued to be performed. Confucian scholars were given exemption from tax. The exclusion of the scholars from high office in favour of non-Chinese, however, antagonised everyone. Fearful of placing too much power in Chinese hands, the Yuan entrusted tax collection to Muslims and central Asian merchants. In fact, as long as you were not Chinese, you could find a senior position and Uighurs, Khitans, Tibetans and even the Venetian Marco Polo succeeded in doing so. Muslims rebuilt the capital, a Persian astronomer worked at court, Muslim and Persian doctors worked in the newly founded hospitals and at the Imperial Academy of Medicine. In fact, the Chinese felt like an inferior class in their own empire. Venetian merchant, Marco Polo, who visited China between 1275 and 1295, wrote of the feelings of the Chinese people:

'All the Cathaians detested the rule of the Great Khan because he set over them Tartars [Mongols], or still more frequently Saracens, whom they could not endure, for they treated them just like slaves.'

73

Society was segmented into four classes for legal purposes: Mongols at the top, followed in order by non-Chinese, northern Chinese, who had experience of Mongol rule and, at the bottom, southern Chinese. Chinese were not allowed to keep or manufacture weapons, including even vegetable knives and meat choppers, only one of which was allowed between ten families. Curfews were imposed and all events at which Chinese might assemble, such as fairs, were banned. An agent was allocated to every ten households in order to prevent discussion or thoughts of rebellion and the Chinese were not permitted to indulge in any sport or pastime that might develop their fighting skills.

For the ordinary person and the peasant there were many hardships. The Mongols imposed punitive taxes and many lost their lands which the Mongols converted to pasture from arable or let go to waste. In fact, in the northwest this contributed to the creation of dust-bowl conditions and encroaching desert. A sixth of the peasantry was starving but many also lost their freedom, forced into serfdom or slavery and transported great distances from home to work. Forced labour was increased to provide workers for imperial construction projects. They were allowed, however, to worship their gods as before. Marco Polo reported the emperor as saying:

> 'There are four prophets who are worshipped and to whom all the world does reverence. The Christians say their god was Jesus Christ, the Saracens Muhammed, the Jews Moses and the idolaters Sakyamuni Burkhan [Buddha], who was the first to be represented as God in the form of an idol. And I do reverence to all four, so that I may be sure of doing it to him who is greatest in heaven and truest; and to him do I pray for aid.'

The emperor had a letter written in Latin to the Pope in Rome, inviting a hundred missionaries to China. They failed to materialise, however, and nor did the Pope reply to the letter.

A Nestorian archbishopric was set up under the auspices of an 'Office for Christian Clergy' and Nestorians served at court. But mosques were also built and Muslim communities grew. However, under the influence of a young Tibetan monk, Drogön Chögyal Phagpa, nephew of the founder of the Lama sect in Tibet, Kublai came to favour Buddhism over Daoism. He recognised the young man as temporal leader in Tibet and the Tibetan acknowledged the emperor as his spiritual equal. Lama temples were built and there was an increase in the number of Buddhist establishments, maintained by around a quarter of a million monks and nuns.

There is little doubt that the economy that had flourished during Song times was seriously damaged during this period of alien rule and it would be many centuries before it would recover. The Mongols, like the Jurchen and the Khitan before them, endeavoured to maintain the circulation of currency, including paper money, and allowed the conversion of Song paper currency into Yuan currency. By the fourteenth century, however, the economy was crippled by runaway inflation.

Meanwhile, agriculture flourished as a result of improved irrigation and drainage. Cotton, which had been cultivated since the Song era, was made into high quality textile. Ceramics, too, continued to be produced to a very high standard, sometimes using craftsmen from nations defeated by the Mongols.

Kublai Khan oversaw numerous building projects – palaces, pleasure gardens, pavilions and lakes turned Beijing into a capital that was the equal of any from past dynasties. He founded an observatory and introduced a new calendar lasting 365.2 days. He dispatched expeditions to discover the source of the Yellow River, re-constructed and extended the Grand Canal northwards, linking the Yellow River with the capital. This part of the canal took an astonishing two and a half million workers to build. The paved highway on its embankments stretched some 1,090 miles from Hangzhou to Beijing. It was a journey that at the time took forty days.

The Mongol postal service that connected the farthest extents of the Mongol empire with the rest of it was extended into China and consisted of 50,000 horses, thousands of oxen, 4,000 carts and 6,000 boats. Kublai Khan wanted the citizens of his vast empire, who all spoke different languages, to be able to communicate. To this end, he required an alphabet to be created and appointed Drogön Chögyal Phagpa, his guru and spiritual adviser, to undertake this task. Phagpa modified traditional Tibetan script and invented a new set of a thousand characters known as 'Phags-pa script' or 'square writing' which became the official writing system of the empire. There was resistance to it, however, and although it appeared on imperial decrees, paper money and in other places until the fourteenth century, it never gained full acceptance.

The novel and the drama had begun to be popular during Song times, but it was under Mongol rule that these two art-forms flourished, probably as a consequence of the fact that scholars, denied official positions, had to find another outlet for their talents. During this time, one of China's greatest dramatists, Guan Hanqing (c. 1241–1320) was writing comedies and tragedies, such as *Gan Tian Dong Di Dou E Yuan* (*The Injustice to Dou E*).

The Decline of the Yuan Empire

As he grew older, Kublai Khan's health deteriorated. Official portraits show the fit and healthy man of 1260 turning into a grossly overweight figure. He suffered from gout and rheumatism and was plunged into depression by the deaths firstly of his beloved and influential wife, Chabi, and then of his son, the Heir Apparent, Zhen Jin in 1285. The great Mongol Empire, stretching at one point from China to Eastern Europe, was declining just as he was. He waged disastrous campaigns against Annam, Vietnam and Japan. The great fleet he dispatched against the Japanese was destroyed by storms and determined Japanese resistance. His authority as Great Khan had come under threat almost since he had taken the Chinese throne and the other three khanates had effectively become independent of him.

Kublai Khan died in 1294 and his body was transported back to Mongolia where it was buried in an unknown grave. After him, there followed a series of incompetent and debauched rulers. By the mid-fourteenth century, the Mongols who ruled in Beijing were very far removed from those who had conquered all of China a hundred years previously. They had been born south of the Wall, far from the steppe, and had never taken part in the extraordinary campaigns that had brought the Mongol Empire success beyond its wildest dreams and put Kublai Khan on the imperial throne of China. Once again in China, secret societies came to the fore, working for the overthrow of the Yuan and a return to Chinese rule. It would be a member of one such society who would single-handedly change the course of Chinese history and found the next dynasty – the Ming.

Ming Dynasty (1368 to 1644)

Re-unification

In 1100, the population of the Northern Song Empire had been around 100 million. The impact of the Jurchen conquest, however, led to a decline in the population, to about 53 million in the north by 1207. This combined with the population of the Southern Song – around 65 million – gave China a total population of 120 million before the Mongol conquest. In 1290, however, the registered population of the empire – decimated by the Mongol invasion – was down to 60 million, a figure that remained unchanged a century later. This stagnation in population may not have been altogether the fault of the Mongols. The improvements in communications across vast distances in Asia will inevitably have facilitated the spread of deadly plagues and diseases. In the three months after the first siege of Kaifeng in 1232, for instance, half a million people died in an epidemic. Rule was also, more often than not, backed up with terror and violence, something the Jurchens and the Mongols understood perhaps far better than written laws and regulations. This will also have contributed to the reduced population. China, however, had once again survived an exceedingly difficult period – centuries of alien rule and fragmentation – with its institutions, customs and culture intact. Confucian teaching had continued, artists and writers had carried on working according to their traditions and Chinese rituals were still being enacted.

The next emperor – the first commoner in fifteen centuries to achieve that position – would be one of the most significant figures in Chinese history. Zhu Yuanzhang was born into poverty in a village in Zhongli (modern-day Fengyang in Anhui Province). His family was so poor that his parents had to give away several of his older siblings. When he was sixteen, there was a flood when the Yellow River broke its banks, a catastrophe that brought famine, plague and epidemic to the region, killing all of Zhu Yuanzhang's family, apart from one brother. He was left destitute but fulfilled a promise he had made to his parents by becoming a novice monk at the Huangjue Temple, a local Buddhist monastery. Life at the monastery was no less difficult and the monks were sent out to beg for the means of survival. Zhu spent several years roaming east-central China, witnessing at first hand the hardships endured by the peasants. Several years later, after he had returned to the monastery, it was burned to the ground by Yuan troops who were intent on suppressing local rebellions.

In 1352, he enlisted with one of the many rebel groups that had risen against the Mongols. His group was affiliated with the Red Turbans, a society created by followers of White Lotus, a Buddhist sect whose teachings partly derived from Manichaeism and that worshipped the 'Unborn or Eternal Venerable Mother' who, it was said, would gather all her children into one family at the millennium. It also predicted the imminent arrival of the future Buddha Maitreya, a successor to the historic Sakyamuni Buddha. It was said that the Buddha Maitreya would appear when the Dharma – the teachings of Buddha – had been forgotten on earth. The name 'Red Turban' was coined in response to the rebels' customary headgear.

The rebellions began on the coast of Zhejiang and spread. Han Shantong, leader of White Lotus, planned an armed rebellion in 1351, but his plan got out, leading to his arrest and execution. His son, Han Lin'er, stepped into his shoes while other rebels formed the Southern Red Turbans south of the Yangtze. Amongst the prominent leaders were Xu Shouhui (ruled 1351–60), ruler of Tianwan, who proclaimed himself emperor and Chen Youliang (1320–63) who declared himself 'King of Han' in 1357 and later emperor. Zhu Yuanzhang was rapidly promoted until, in 1355, he became leader, seen as a defender of Confucianism against the Mongols. In 1356, he captured Nanjing which he made the base for his subsequent campaigns and which would become his capital as emperor.

By 1358, when central and southern China were under the control of different rebel factions, Zhu began to eliminate rivals within his own Red Turban faction. In 1363, he defeated Chen Youliang in one of the biggest naval battles in history – the Battle of Lake Poyang. Chen died in another battle a month later. In 1367, Zhu defeated the Kingdom of Dazhou, ruled by Zhang Shicheng (ruled 1354–67). The kingdom included much of the Yangtze River delta and the Song capital of Hangzhu. The seizure of this territory gave Zhu control over the lands to the north and south of the Yangtze and other warlords surrendered to him.

By now, his imperial ambitions were clear and, to ensure that he had no rivals, he is said to have had Han Lin'er drowned, preventing him from becoming emperor, as had seemed likely. Finally, on 20 January 1368, Zhu proclaimed himself Emperor of the Ming Dynasty, adopting Hongwu (ruled 1368–98) as his imperial title, although often known as Taizu. Emperor Hongwu now set about driving the Mongols of the Yuan Dynasty from China, sending his army north towards the Yuan capital at Khanbaliq (present-day Beijing). The Mongols did not put up a fight, the court fleeing instead to Mongolia. The last Yuan-controlled province, Yunnan, was captured in 1381 and the Middle Kingdom was re-unified under the rule of the Ming Dynasty.

The Hongwu Emperor: the First Ming Ruler

With Nanjing named capital of the Ming Empire, for the first time China was to be ruled from a city located to the south of the Yangtze River and the population of the new capital rapidly increased – from 100,000 to around a million. The emperor built thirty miles of walls around the city and constructed palaces and government buildings. Hongwu determined to create a world that was as far removed as possible from the violent, decadent one that had gone before in the last years of the Yuan Dynasty. He wanted his people to observe a strict social hierarchy, obeying and showing respect for superiors. Naturally, the emperor, with the Mandate of Heaven, sat at the pinnacle of that hierarchy. Officials had to kneel when addressing him and were punished when they failed to do so. He believed that by observing the social hierarchy, living harmoniously together and embracing traditional moral standards, the lives of his people would be subject to less government intrusion. In fact, imperial guidelines to the proper way to live were posted in every village, encouraging people to conduct themselves according to Confucian values, to show proper respect for parents, elders and ancestors and to live a peaceful life. He assigned to the better-off villagers the tasks of applying justice, providing policing and collecting taxes, avoiding the problem of greedy tax collectors.

He was keen to lighten the burden that government had placed on the peasantry, commissioning a registration of the population and all cultivated land so that tax and other liabilities could be more fairly allocated. He cut government costs where possible. For instance, he made his 2 million-strong army more or less self-supporting by distributing land to soldiers' families to farm. The most pressing task of the new government, however, was the re-establishment of agriculture, especially in the north, which had not only been devastated by the Mongols but had also endured famines and floods for decades. Peasants received encouragement from the government. Any land that they restored to agriculture was given to them and for the first three years the produce was exempted from taxation. A decree stipulated that a proportion of all land was to be given over to cash crops – mulberry trees for silk, and cotton and hemp, for example – and in this way the raw materials were produced for textile crafts while at the same time they provided an income for the peasants working the land. Taxation in the form of forced labour continued under Ming rule, adjusted according to the number of adult males living in a household.

Dykes and canals that had been neglected by the Mongols were repaired and brought back into use and tens of thousands of reservoirs were constructed or restored. Hongwu initiated a campaign of reforestation in order to provide wood for shipbuilding and during his thirty-year reign it is estimated that around a billion trees were planted.

If the burden was lessened for the poor, the commercial and scholarly elites were less fortunate. They had to endure punitive taxes, especially in the wealthy southeast from which numerous well-off families moved, a great many of them settling in Nanjing. Hongwu based his government on that employed by the Tang, re-introducing Confucianism but he, himself, took control of many areas of government, abolishing the position of prime minister and personally taking charge of the six ministries – civil offices, rites, revenue, war, punishments and works. He worked with the help of a group of ministers, known as Grand Secretaries, who were somewhat like a cabinet.

Hongwu restored the examination system and it became a remarkable process. In every city, a large building was constructed for the examinations. In the middle of these buildings were around 4,000 cells, completely shut off from one another and large enough to contain just a desk and a person. The exams were carried out on the same three days everywhere in the Middle Kingdom, candidates writing from sunrise to sunset, behind locked doors, having been searched on entry to ensure that they were not concealing books or papers on their persons; the punishment for cheating was severe. The subject matter became highly formalised and was confined to the Five Classics and the Four Books that made up the orthodox version of Confucianism. All submitted papers were anonymous, marked in such a way that the candidate could be recognised but not by the examiners. At the end of the process, a book was published throughout the entire empire containing the names of successful candidates and the best papers on each subject. In 1371, however, Taizu was displeased by the quality of the 120 *jinshi* chosen in the examination and he suspended the process for ten years.

Suspicious of all around him, Hongwu banned all secret societies and established the *Jinyi Wei*, a secret police force to spy on his civil servants and to root out dissent. In the next fourteen years, 30,000 lost their lives and later purges of the opposition accounted for around 70,000 lives. Hongwu saw it as his duty to expunge evil and wrongdoing from the world which led to piles of corpses. He wrote:

'In the morning I punish a few; by evening others commit the same crime. I punish these in the evening and by the next morning again there are violations. Although the corpses of the first have not been removed, already others follow in their path. The harsher the punishment, the more the violations. Day and night I cannot rest. This is a situation that cannot be helped. If I enact lenient punishments, these persons will engage in still more evil practices. Then how could the people outside the government lead peaceful lives? What a difficult situation this is! If I punish these persons, I am regarded as a tyrant. If I am lenient towards them, the law becomes ineffective, order deteriorates, and people deem me an incapable ruler.'

(Transl. Lily Hwa in *Chinese Civilisation: a Sourcebook*, ed. Patricia Buckley Ebrey, New York, The Free Press, 1993)

Thus the more open Song system of government was replaced by one that was centralised and decidedly autocratic. Much of the power of the state rested in the emperor's hands and the business of government was conducted behind closed doors and monitored by his secret police force. The emperor's advocacy of Confucian principles contrasted dramatically with this government style and the cruelty he often displayed. Torture was routinely used, including flaying and slow slicing (*lingchi*) – the removal of portions of the body with a knife over an extended period of time. These practices, understandably, led to feelings of insecurity in the empire and the formation of factions. The emperor especially feared the palace eunuchs whom he deliberately kept out of government. Although he limited their advancement – decreeing, for instance, that they should remain illiterate – he did not abolish the role within his palace, a decision that later Ming emperors would regret as they became mired in in-fighting between eunuchs and officials.

There is little doubt that, despite his astonishing achievements, Hongwu's humble origins and lack of education left him with feelings of inadequacy and, to some extent, these factors possibly explain his un-Confucian behaviour. When he died in 1398, at the age of 70, Hongwu was laid to rest in a characteristically simple funeral although thirty-eight concubines were immolated with him, as had been the custom of the Mongols who had preceded him.

The Failed Legacy of Hongwu

Hongwu wished his legacy to remain intact, but within a century that legacy began to be dismantled. His heir was Jianwen (ruled 1398–1402), his fifteen-year-old grandson. However, within three years of the teenager coming to the throne, his uncle, the late Emperor Hongwu's fourth son, who became known as the Yongle Emperor (ruled 1402–24), usurped the throne by civil war. He moved the imperial capital to Beijing where a programme of palace-building by hundreds of thousands of workers was instituted. A new imperial residence, the Forbidden City, was built over a period of fifteen years, forming the heart of the government district, known as the Imperial City. Nanjing, meanwhile, was demoted to the status of 'secondary' capital, responsible for fiscal matters and for ensuring that the north of the empire shared in the tax revenues collected in the wealthy south. An extension of the Grand Canal was undertaken, a prodigious feat of engineering that took the canal through a series of fifteen locks over western Shandong. This took the canal to its greatest height – 138 feet – which was achieved due to the invention in 984 by government official and engineer Qiao Weiyo of the double-gate system, known as the pound lock, the lock that is used on canals and rivers today. This extension allowed the capital to be supplied with grain.

But other elements of Hongwu's legacy came under threat in the decades following his demise. Unpaid service had played an important role in his society but this limited the sources of revenue for tax-collectors, leading to the type of abuses the Ming Dynasty's first emperor had tried so hard to avoid. Furthermore, the local requirement to deliver taxes without being paid for the time and the provision of other free services soon proved untenable. Reforms introduced a more orthodox financial tax. During the Ming Dynasty, the supply of money – both paper and coin – became a problem and eventually paper money was abolished and silver ingots became the unit of currency. Hongwu's self-supporting army also failed to live up to his ambition. Desertion and sale of their farmland by soldiers devastated the army, leading emperors to create mercenary forces in order to protect the empire.

Honwu's desire to keep the eunuchs as far from power as possible also eventually failed. Within decades of his death, palace eunuchs were involved in all aspects of government and, by the last century of the Ming Dynasty, there were some 70,000 eunuchs in service throughout the empire. Their power reached its zenith during the reign of Emperor Wanli (ruled 1572–1620) who, becoming disillusioned by the arguments between officials and their disdain for his decisions, simply went on strike, ignoring matters of government and appointments of officials. The situation continued for years and eunuchs ran the country while Wanli became so obese he could neither stand up nor walk unaided.

Despite the problems of later years, the population of China grew during the Ming Dynasty, from between 60 and 80 million to between 150 and 200 million. Cheap water transport helped small communities to specialise in cash crops and market towns developed across the empire. Individual regions began to specialise in agricultural production – the Yangtze River delta becoming known for the production of cotton and silk, for example, while Fuijan on the coast specialised in tobacco and sugar cane.

Expansion

The traditional area of the Middle Kingdom was extended by the Ming Dynasty rulers. The territories of Yunnan and Guizhou were fully subsumed by the empire in 1381. 200,000 colonists flooded into the area and further influxes during the fifteenth and sixteenth centuries brought another 500,000 settlers. Naturally, this brought a change to the ethnic make-up of the region which was populated by only around three million people in the mid-fourteenth century and only around half of those are thought to have been Han. Migrants came from all over China, but they were united by the knowledge that, although they may have spoken with different dialects and enjoyed different customs and traditions, they were Han Chinese.

In such areas as the southwest, where there was a large Chinese population, taxes were collected and the law was enforced by regular officials, but where indigenous tribes were in the majority, the Ming recognised the traditional rights of hereditary rulers to govern their territories in return for tribute payments and for supporting the government when problems arose. Manchuria was also colonised and populated by settlers and, in the northwest, the Ming established control of Hami, the first station on the Old Silk Road, although that was as far as they went into Central Asia.

The Mongols remained a threat in the north and, in the fourteenth century, to protect the country against them, the Ming revisited the notion of the Great Wall. It became even more pressing after their defeat at the hands of the Oirats, the westernmost group of Mongols, at the Battle of Tumu in 1449. The constant incursions from Mongolia and Manchuria were costly and, to protect the empire, frontier walls were constructed along the northern border. The Ming construction was of bricks and stone, unlike the earlier effort of the Qin who used compacted earth. There were up to 25,000 watchtowers and, over the years, the Ming devoted considerable resources to the repair and reinforcement of the Wall.

These movements and displacements of peoples did not take place without problems. Often Chinese settlers would treat the native peoples of the areas in which they had settled as little more than slaves and the resentful locals would terrorise the Chinese whenever they could. Between 1464 and 1466 there were attacks on heavily populated cities by Miao and Yao tribes. The army was sent in to pacify the areas and to execute the leaders of the uprisings, 800 of whom were beheaded in Beijing.

The familiar superior attitude of the Chinese towards other nations was displayed by the tribute system established by Hongwu. He sent out envoys with a manifesto that said:

'Since the Song Dynasty lost the throne and Heaven cut off their sacrifice, the Yuan Dynasty arose from the desert to enter and rule over China for more than a hundred years, when Heaven, wearied of their misgovernment and debauchery, thought fit to

turn their fate also to ruin, and the affairs of China were in a state of disorder for eighteen years. But when the nation began to arouse itself, We, a simple peasant of Huai-yu, conceived the patriotic idea to save the people, and it pleased the creator to grant that Our civil and military officers effected their passage eastward to the left side of the River... We have established peace in the empire and restored the old boundaries of our Middle Land. We were also selected by our people to occupy the imperial throne of China... We have sent officers to all foreign kingdoms with the manifesto. Although We are not equal in Our wisdom to our ancient rulers whose virtue was recognised all over the universe, We cannot but let the world know Our intention to maintain peace within the four seas. It is on this ground alone that we have issued this manifesto.'
(*China and the Roman Orient*, F. Hirth Chicago, Ares Publishers, 1998))

Many responded to the manifesto and sent tribute – amongst them, Korea, Annam, Siam, Cambodia, Borneo, Java, Sumatra and Syria. Envoys also arrived from Holland and Italy.

The majority of the trade carried out by the Ming was by sea and by this time the ships they were sailing across the western oceans had developed greatly, described by one observer as being 'like houses'. There were maritime expeditions, such as the one ordered by the Yongle Emperor in 1405 in which the Muslim Hui-Chinese eunuch, admiral and diplomat, Zheng He (1371–1433) set out for the west at the head of a great fleet carrying 28,000 men. During his life, Zheng He commanded voyages to Southeast Asia, South Asia, the Middle East, Somalia and the Swahili coast. There were several reasons for the seven expeditions Zhen He undertook. The emperor sought to establish a Chinese presence on the high seas, he wished to control trade and to extend his lucrative tribute system. It has been suggested that the voyages also provided an opportunity to search for the previous emperor Zhu Yunwen who some thought had escaped death and fled when the Yongle Emperor had usurped his throne. Trade and tribute were established with thirty countries. Of course, this attempt to prove that the emperor did, indeed, have dominion over 'All Under Heaven' was completely lacking in substance and only from China's closest neighbours was the proper subordination forthcoming. Given the Chinese Empire's sinocentric view of the rest of the world, however, it was the only way it knew how to relate to other states.

China's maritime forays into the wider world – and especially those of Zheng He – were undoubtedly remarkable achievements, both in terms of technical skill and logistical prowess. However, the succeeding emperors, Hongxi (ruled 1424–25) and Xuande (ruled 1425–35) believed the expeditions to be too costly and even thought that they might be damaging the Chinese state. Hongxi prohibited further exploration and, in the years to come, knowledge of Zheng He's voyages was suppressed. The timing was ironic because, of course, just as China brought a halt to exploration of the southern oceans, others were gearing up for the great age of discovery. The Chinese left the way clear for the Arabs, the Portuguese and, later, the British.

Art and Literature

It was a similar story in the world of art and literature. Just at the moment when Europe was witnessing the birth of the Renaissance, a dynamic period of exploration, discovery and advancement in almost every field, the Chinese were, in reaction to the century of Mongol rule, casting envious eyes at their past instead of launching themselves into the future. Understandably, the intention was to reject anything that was alien and restore traditional Chinese customs and practices. It was true of the Ming approach to government that harked back to their Tang and Song predecessors but it was also evident in the fields of art and culture.

In painting, the court dictated styles in the arts. The Ming emperors ordered that painters return to the didactic and realistic representation of nature that had been evident in the style of the Southern Song Imperial Painting Academy. Artists were expected to convey the majestic, benevolent and virtuous nature of the new dynasty by painting large landscapes, flowers and birds as well as figural narratives. Amongst the numerous famous artists of the period were Ni Zan (1301–74), Shen Zhou (1427–1509), Wen Zhengming (1470–1559) and Qiu Ying (c. 1494-c. 1552). The Zhe (Zhejiang Province) school of painting emulated the descriptive, ink-wash style of the Southern Song while the expressive calligraphic styles of Yuan scholar-painters were being explored by the Wu (Suzhou) school. Ming Dynasty artists could make a good living from their work and their paintings were much sought-after by collectors. There were even guides to help the connoisseur of the arts, such as a 1635 book by Liu Tong (c. 1593–1637) that gave advice on how to tell the difference between real and fake works of art.

Literature also flourished during this period and the publishing industry was exploding. In fact, the Italian Jesuit missionary, Matteo Ricci (1552–1610), who lived in China from 1579 until his death thirty-one years later, reflected on 'the exceedingly large numbers of books in circulation here and the ridiculously low prices at which they are sold'. Although short stories had been popular since the Tang Dynasty, the novel form began to be explored. After all, there was a large audience – women in educated families, merchants and shop clerks – that was educated enough to read and understand the vernacular Chinese that was used in some forms of literature and the performing arts. Writer and poet, Feng Menglong (1574–1645), published collections of humorous, vernacular short stories.

Two of the works considered to be the Four Great Classical Novels of China were published during the Ming period – the Robin Hood-style novel *Shuihu Zhuan* (*Water Margin*), attributed to Shi Nai'an (c. 1296–1372) and *Journey to the West* by Wu Cheng'en (c. 1500–1582) working under the pen name 'Sheyang Hermit'. More practical works were also available, including lavishly illustrated home reference books that provided information and advice on everything from the way to correctly perform a funeral to multiplication tables. Religious tracts, school textbooks and costly editions of the Confucian classics for examination candidates were also published. In drama, too, there were imaginative and successful works including one of the most famous plays in Chinese history – *The Peony Pavilion* by Tang Xianzu (1550–1616).

The Yongle Emperor commissioned one of the most audacious

literary projects ever mounted – the compilation of the Yongle Encyclopedia (*Yongle Dadian*) which in its day was the largest general encyclopedia in the world. More than two thousand scholars were engaged on this mammoth work for four years. Rare books were sent from across the Middle Kingdom and copied before being sent back. It amounted to 11,095 volumes but proved too long to print. Two copies were, however, made by hand. Sadly, fewer than 400 volumes have survived.

In ceramics the Ming Dynasty saw a remarkable period of innovation, with new designs, shapes and colours. Foreign influences were in evidence, especially from Islamic countries, with the Yongle Emperor enjoying the unusual shapes inspired by Islamic metalwork, for instance. While Xuande occupied the dragon throne, new glazing techniques led to crisper lines and ceramics from this time are now considered amongst the finest of the Ming Dynasty. Furthermore, in the later Ming, porcelain was exported around the world in vast quantities. During the reign of the Wanli Emperor, the Jingdezhen and Dehua porcelain factories became centres for the production of large-scale porcelain exports to Europe.

Religion and Philosophy

During the Ming Dynasty, there was little change in the way people worshipped. Buddhism, Daoism, ancestor worship and Chinese folk religion remained predominant. As the West began to look beyond its borders, religious people saw opportunities to expand their flocks amongst the vast populations of the Orient. Jesuit missionaries such as Matteo Ricci and the Flemish missionary, Nicolas Trigault (1577–1628), arrived, as did parties of Dominicans and Franciscans. It took Matteo Ricci twenty years to make his way from Macau to Beijing where he was well received at court, despite the opposition of the mandarins who may have been irritated by the fact that it was a eunuch who introduced the missionary to the emperor. The emperor, however, took a liking to the Italian, generously providing him with a house and a maintenance allowance. Ricci remained in China until his death in 1610 by which time he had earned the respect of many, including officials. He worked alongside the

Chinese mathematician, astronomer and agronomist, Xu Guangqi (1562–1633), to translate the Greek mathematical work, *Euclid's Elements*, into Chinese in 1607.

The Jesuits helped in the reform of the Chinese calendar and introduced western science and technology to China, although this caused problems for some Chinese who were suspicious of the Christians and their religion. The Nanjing Religious Incident of 1616 to 1622 gave these Confucian traditionalists a small victory when it was decided that western science derived from a superior Chinese model. This decision was soon overturned, however, and western missionaries were once again working with the Imperial Astronomical Board.

The most influential rationalist Neo-Confucianist in China during the Song period had been Zhu Xi (1130–1200) and the Ming court and the Chinese literati embraced his thinking and his notion of Neo-Confucianism. To Zhu Xi's mind, an understanding of moral principles could only be achieved through years of study. In the middle of the Ming period, however, his version of Confucianism was challenged by the scholar official, Wang Yangming (1472–1529). In Wang's philosophy, anyone could become as wise as the ancient sages, regardless of his or her social or economic background. Universal principles existed in everyone's mind; it was merely a matter of removing obstacles such as material greed from the mind and to experience life to arrive at wisdom equivalent to that of Confucius and Mencius. In fact, he controversially claimed, their writings were merely guides and could even be flawed.

Naturally, conservative Confucianists were horrified by Wang's seditious message and he was often sent far away from the capital to deal with military matters. However, his ideas began to take hold and people started to question some of the fundamental tenets of traditional Confucianism, especially the social hierarchy. A number of his followers in the next century were imprisoned for spreading what were viewed as 'dangerous ideas' such as the notion that women were the equal of men and should be given the opportunity to gain a better education.

Decline of the Ming Dynasty

The end of the Ming Dynasty was presaged by a fiscal crisis. By the early seventeenth century, the government was virtually bankrupt. There were a number of reasons for this. The cost of maintaining the imperial family – some 23,000 people by the time of Emperor Wanli – was becoming burdensome on the royal coffers as were military campaigns, against Korea and Japan, for example. Added to this was the fact that peasants were losing their lands and wealthy landlords were paying as little tax as possible.

The meteorological phenomenon known as the 'Little Ice Age' in the early seventeenth century brought ecological calamities that could not be managed from the centre due to lack of funds. Bad harvests resulted, followed by famines. The famine of 1627 to 1628 in northern Shaanxi led to mass desertions from the army and soon these men formed gangs that roamed the countryside, stealing whatever they could find. The gangs grew in size, spreading their mayhem east and west of Shaanxi. By 1636, they had become organised and were being led by two men. In the north, Li Zicheng (1606-c. 1645), a former shepherd who had also worked in a wine shop and as an ironworker's apprentice was in control. Meanwhile, in the area between the Yellow and Yangtze rivers, former soldier Zhang Xianzhong (1606–47) was the leader.

One of the major problems at the time was the cessation of the flow of silver into China. The Japanese banned traders from Macau from entering Nagasaki, thus preventing the traders from bringing silver back with them. To make matters worse, tensions rose between the Chinese and the Spanish in Manila in the Philippines, resulting in a conflict in which more than 20,000 lost their lives. Trade between the two nations ended and another source of silver was alienated. The Chinese economy collapsed and many were unable to pay their taxes. By the end of the sixteenth century, eunuchs, serving as tax collectors, were being sent into China's cities to make their levies. They were ruthless in their approach, arresting and even killing defaulters, and their oppressive arrogance stirred up revolt amongst the people. In 1600, textile workers rose up against the tax collectors, the first time in Chinese history that urban workers had revolted. Discontent and rebellion began to spread and the death toll was staggering. In 1642, when a band of rebels broke the dykes of the Yellow River, the subsequent flood and famine claimed hundreds of thousands of lives. Epidemics also decimated the population during these decades.

Meanwhile, the rebels were gaining ground, with Li Zicheng taking Hubei, Henan and Shaanxi. In April 1644, he entered Beijing. With the imperial army fleeing or surrendering, the last Ming ruler, Emperor Chongzhen (ruled 1628–44) climbed Prospect Hill behind his palace and hanged himself from a locust tree with his own girdle. Both Li and Zhang, who had in the meantime taken Sichuan, proclaimed dynasties, establishing governments and even launching civil service examinations and minting coins. The country was still largely unstable, however, with looting and civil disorder continuing unabated. Once again, an army from beyond the Great Wall in the north arrived on the scene to exploit the weakness of the two governments, seize power and restore order to the empire.

The Ming Dynasty: In Conclusion

The Ming era was the only extended period of native rule over the entirety of China from the fall of the Northern Song in 1126 to the demise of the Manchus in 1912. It is a period that is often criticised for a number of reasons. The rulers of the dynasty, for instance, failed to rule effectively, lacking control over the eunuchs, the economy and outside forces such as the Mongols and the Japanese. Internal tensions between monarchs and their bureaucrats frequently paralysed the machinery of state.

While Europe was forging ahead with astonishing innovation and decisive social change, the Chinese Empire under the Ming stagnated, inhibiting innovation and entrepreneurship, as demonstrated by China's withdrawal of its ships from the oceans just when Europe's maritime nations were embarking on the Age of Discovery, sending their ships to Asia and the Americas. Moreover, China, the birthplace of printing, gunpowder and the compass, handed the initiative in scientific and technological development to the Europeans. As one observer has noted:

'From the seventeenth century onwards, the Chinese became increasingly dazzled by European technological expertise, having experienced a period of amnesia regarding their own achievements. When the Chinese were shown a mechanical clock by Jesuit missionaries, they were awestruck. They had forgotten that it was they who had invented mechanical clocks in the first place!'
Robert Temple – *The Genius of China: 300 Years of Science, Discovery and Invention*, Robert Temple, London, Andre Deutsch, 2007

On the plus side, however, the increase in population, growing commercialisation, an extensive publishing industry and local control of community life all helped the ordinary Chinese to develop a sense of common history and identity. It also has to be acknowledged that the Ming emperors did succeed in maintaining a degree of peace over their vast empire and population for some two centuries, no mean feat in those warlike times.

Qing Dynasty (1644 to 1912)

Rise of the Manchus
Following the demise of the Ming Dynasty, a new ruling dynasty emerged, once again from the forests and plains beyond the Great Wall. The Manchus can be traced back to the ancient Sushen people who were famous for their use of wooden bows and arrows that they used to pay tribute to the Chinese King Shun (ruled c.2255-c.2195 BC) during the Three Sovereigns and Five Emperors period (c. 2852–2070 BC) as well as during the Zhou Dynasty. They were known as 'Jurchen' until the tenth century and were affiliated to the Khitan Empire that later became the Liao Dynasty. Jurchen leader Wanyan Aguda (ruled 1115–23) established the Jin Dynasty as Emperor Taizu in northern Manchuria. The Jin defeated the Song in 1141 and ruled northern China until 1234 when they were overrun by the Mongols. The Jurchens began to pay tribute to the Ming emperors.

In 1616, the important Jurchen chieftain, Nurhaci (ruled 1616–26) united various Jurchen tribes and declared himself Khan, founding the Jin Dynasty, commonly known as the Later Jin. Nurhaci spent thirty years overthrowing Ming rule in Manchuria and recorded many defeats of Ming, Mongol, Korean and other Jurchen armies. He enlisted the entire population of his Manchu state in four military units – later eight – each of which was signified by a coloured banner. He also ordered the creation of a Manchu script for writing. This was used in the adaptation of Ming legal codes, introducing Chinese administrative practices. In 1618, as society in Ming China was unravelling, Nurhaci attacked the Liaodong area in the northeast of the empire. All men captured were forced to serve in his army as well as to adopt the Manchu hairstyle – the front of the head shaved and the remainder of the hair worn as a long plait or queue.

Nurhaci's successor, his son Hong Taiji (ruled 1626–43), expanded the Manchu domain, as Ming generals defected to his side with their armies and Mongols also enlisted. In 1636, Hong Taiji changed the dynasty name from Jin to Qing, meaning 'pure'. In 1644, when Li Zicheng took Beijing, General Wu Sangui (1612–78) opened the gates of the Great Wall at the Shanhai Pass which is located at the Wall's eastern end and allowed the Qing army to enter China. Considering joining the rebel forces of Li, Wu had entered into negotiations with the Qing Prince Regent Dorgon (1612–50) on hearing that his concubine and her father had been arrested. Dorgon's troops poured through the gates and onwards to Beijing which they occupied only a month after the suicide of the emperor. Li retreated to Xi'an where he was killed a year later when the Manchus captured the city.

The Ming generals had hoped that the Manchus would do no more than serve as mercenaries in their armies but it quickly became evident that they were here to stay and wanted to rule. The eunuchs were mostly expelled and huge tracts of land were confiscated in order to support the large Manchu force. Every man had to adopt the Manchu hairstyle and, if he failed to do so within ten days, he was executed. It was humiliating for the Chinese, but they had no option but to comply.

Rebels continued to emerge and maintain the struggle against the Manchus to prevent them penetrating south of the Yangtze. Where there was resistance, however, they were ruthless. At Yangzhou, 800,000 people are said to have been massacred after the city fell. The southern gentry were faced with surrender and peace or terrible violence and it took fifteen years for the Qing to subdue them. The last Ming pretender, Zhu Youlang, Prince of Gui (1623–62) was hunted down and assassinated in Burma. In 1673, Wu Sangui led the last serious attempt to cast off the Qing yoke but, after eight years of conflict, known as the Revolt of the Three Feudatories, and the death of Wu, the revolt was quashed. The Qing now ruled All Under Heaven.

Kangxi, Yongzheng and Qianlong

From 1669 to 1799, China was, astonishingly, ruled by only three emperors. Kangxi (ruled 1661–1722) – Chinese history's longest-reigning emperor – and Qianlong (ruled 1735–96, although still in effective control until his death in 1799) enjoyed especially long reigns. The Kangxi Emperor and the Qianlong Emperor each occupied the throne for a remarkable sixty-one years while, between these two marathon reigns, Yongzheng (ruled 1722–35) occupied the Dragon Throne for thirteen years. They were good and hard-working rulers who, on the whole, eschewed the practice of arbitrary rule, developing the institutions of government and ensuring that systems were put in place to ensure the collection of tax revenue.

Kangxi was the second Qing emperor, ascending to the throne at the age of seven. Until he was fifteen, the effective rulers of China were four regents and his grandmother, Grand Empress Dowager Xiaozhuang (1613–88), the latter a highly respected figure in the annals of Qing history. Kangxi is acknowledged as one of the greatest of all Chinese emperors. Aged just eighteen, he took personal responsibility for the handling of the Three Feudatories Revolt. Immediately afterwards, to preserve his empire, he embarked upon a policy of pacification, softening the Manchu treatment of native Chinese. Hitherto, they had confiscated large tracts of land and treated the peasants more or less as slaves.

Segregation of Chinese and Manchus was practised, with intermarriage forbidden. In the capital, Beijing, Chinese had been expelled from the Forbidden City and forced to live in the southern part of the city. Kangxi relaxed these policies, lowering taxes and prohibiting further land seizure. This served to stimulate agricultural production, providing more tax revenue for the imperial coffers. Increases in the salaries of officials resulted in less corruption. He engaged with Chinese culture, but also displayed an interest in Western technology as well as Western progress in the fields of science and mathematics. He was also the first Chinese emperor to learn to play a Western musical instrument, the spinet. Jesuit missionaries were received at court and he decreed that Christianity would be tolerated as long as converts continued to perform ancestral rites. When a papal legate, Charles-Thomas Maillard de Tournon (1668–1710), refused to allow the celebration of these rites, the emperor began to support other Catholic orders rather than the Jesuits. Furthermore, when de Tournon insisted that the Pope had authority over missionaries and their Chinese converts, Kangxi expelled missionaries who would not do as he said. Meanwhile, he insisted on moral Neo-Confucian orthodoxy being imposed on China, putting the emphasis on 'Sixteen Moral Principles' that he ordered to be read twice monthly in the cities, towns and villages of the empire.

During Kangxi's reign, a dictionary of Chinese characters – the *Kangxi Dictionary* – was compiled, a task that helped to gain the support of Han Chinese scholar bureaucrats who worked on it and who had until then resented Qing rule. He commissioned a *History of the Ming*, one of the collection of official Chinese works known as the *Twenty-Four Histories of China*, as well as the important collection of Tang poetry, the *Quantangshi*, which was produced in 1705. It contained 49,000 poems and is one of the most significant collections of poetry ever assembled.

From records left behind, Kangxi appears to have been a humane ruler who used the death penalty sparingly. He left a *Valedictory Edict* in which he lays out the principles that guided his life. He ends it by saying:

'I have enjoyed the veneration of my country and the riches of the world; there is no object I do not have, nothing I have not experienced. But now that I have reached old age I cannot rest easy for a moment. Therefore, I regard the whole world as a worn-out sandal, and all riches as mud and sand. If I can die without there being an outbreak of trouble, my desires will be fulfilled... I have revealed my entrails and shown my guts, there's nothing left for me to reveal. I will say no more.'

The final years of Kangxi's reign, however, were blighted by a row over the succession. He had 56 children, but only his second son, Yinreng (1674–1725), was born of an empress. Kangxi worshipped the boy but he became unmanageable and mentally unstable. When Yinreng became involved in a plot to unseat Kangxi, he was demoted and the emperor refused to name his successor until he was on his deathbed. At that point, his fourth son, Yongzheng, who was 45 years old, announced that the emperor had chosen him and set about eliminating any brothers or uncles that may have been rivals. The legitimacy of his succession haunted his reign, with many doubting that Kangxi had actually chosen him. He defeated opponents by using a network of spies and ensured that histories from the Kangxi period did not reflect badly on his succession.

Nonetheless, he was a competent ruler, abolishing hereditary servitude and decreeing that every important decision had to be approved by the emperor. He simplified the tax system and was firmly against his own Manchu people being converted to Christianity. He imposed tight control on the civil bureaucracy and restricted the military power of the Manchu aristocracy. Once again, however, there was mystery surrounding the name of the heir to the throne which was kept by Yongzheng in a locked box that was not to be opened until after his death.

Qianlong, Yongzheng's fourth son, was the name that emerged when the box was opened. He revered his grandfather so much that he abdicated so that the length of his reign would not be greater than that of Kangxi. Nonetheless, his reign would be one of the most glorious in Chinese history, the empire expanding to its greatest size ever. Qianlong was an exceedingly conscientious ruler, assiduously applying himself to state affairs for much of the day. He is said to have blended the military skills of a Manchu warrior with the intellect and virtue of a scholar of Confucius. After forty years of his rule, China was, without doubt, the wealthiest and most populous nation on the planet. The final years of his reign were troubled, however, both at home and abroad, largely due to the rapid expansion of the empire.

Under Qianlong's rule, the empire doubled in size and he delineated Greater China, the multi-ethnic state over which the Chinese government presides today. Tibet came under Chinese control, not for the last time in its history, in 1751, with the Dalai Lama being established as ruler, supported by a Chinese garrison. By 1759, the Chinese Empire extended over almost 4.5 million square miles and, in addition to the countries already mentioned, incorporated parts of Russia and Outer Mongolia, stretching as far as the Pamir Mountains in Central Asia. Meanwhile, Korea, Nepal, Burma, Thailand, Vietnam and the Philippines acknowledged Chinese supremacy, becoming tributary states. The island of Taiwan was acquired in 1683.

Like his beloved grandfather, Qianlong was a great patron of the arts. He sponsored such publications as the extraordinary bibliographic project, the compilation of rare works known as the *Siku Quanshu* (*The Four Treasuries*). It was the largest collection of books in Chinese history with more than 3,461 complete works collected and copied by 15,000 scholars in 36,381 volumes, about 2.3 million pages. Sadly, Manchu paranoia resulted in the books being searched for any offensive references to the Manchus or previous foreign rulers of China and the offending volumes – around 2,855 books – were destroyed.

Qing Society

Qing society can be said to have been segmented into five groupings or estates. At the top were the officials and bureaucrats; next came the aristocracy – not a large number of people; then followed the educated *literati*. Below these three groups, the people were divided into two. The first of these were those known as *lingmin*, meaning 'good' or 'noble' commoners. The second were *jianmin*, commoners who were of inferior status and were considered 'ignoble'. Scholars, farmers, artisans and merchants would be included in the first category, while slaves, bondservants, entertainers – including actors and prostitutes – and low-level government officials fell into the latter category. *Jianmin* suffered inequality in many ways, including being prohibited from taking the Imperial Examination.

Qing times brought a more strait-laced approach to life for the subjects of the empire. This trend for conservatism was almost a rebuke to the Ming Dynasty whose pursuit of spontaneity and emotion the Qing intelligentsia saw as weakness that probably contributed to the fall of the dynasty. The rulers had failed to provide the requisite moral leadership and, consequently, the peasantry had lost their respect for authority. The purity and dignity of women now became an issue with record numbers of widows deciding not to remarry. Deviant behaviour was frowned upon and laws were brought in against homosexuality, for example. Many intellectuals rejected drama and fiction that were considered subversive and such novels and plays were frequently proscribed. This did not prevent the publication towards the end of the eighteenth century of the novel *Hongloumeng* (*Dream of the Red Chamber*) by Cao Xueqin (1715 or 1724–1763 or 1764), now recognised as probably the greatest Chinese work of fiction.

During the eighteenth century, the population of the empire doubled and it was also extraordinarily mobile, migrating permanently, or making temporary moves purely temporary. In the latter case, that might have been because those involved were part of the empire's manual labour force. Many Qing subjects also moved overseas, in particular to Southeast Asia, in search of trading opportunities.

Qing China and the Rest of the World

It was in the eighteenth century that China lost the initiative to the West. Before then, in the seventeenth century, the standard of living in China was amongst the highest in the world and the Middle Kingdom was still at the forefront of innovation and invention. A hundred years later, that had all changed and the empire had been left in the wake of the fast-developing European nations. The Portuguese had been the main traders from Europe in the sixteenth century but they had been replaced by the Dutch and then the English, working through the British East India Company and dealing with the Thirteen Hongs, the merchant guild in Guangzhou, the only city, after 1759, in which the ever-protective empire permitted Europeans to trade. To the customary exports of silk and porcelain was added tea for which the eighteenth-century British developed a tremendous thirst. By the start of the nineteenth century, 23 million pounds of tea were being exported annually. It became important to both nations – a tenth of Britain's annual revenue deriving from the tax on tea.

The Chinese, however, still regarded their empire as the Middle Kingdom, the centre of the world, and all non-Chinese as barbarians. One Cantonese Manchu official summed it up neatly at the beginning of the eighteenth century:

'To the extreme west there are the red-haired and western foreigners, a fierce, violent lot, quite unlike the barbarians of the western islands. Among these are the English, the Islamists, the French, the Dutch, the Spaniards and the Portuguese. These are all very fierce nations; their ships are strong and do not fear typhoons; their guns, powder and munitions of war generally are superior to those of China. Their natures are dark, dangerous and inscrutable; wherever they go they spy around with a view to seizing other people's lands.'

The Manchus' restrictions can be put down to a desire to preserve their dynasty in the face of opposition from overseas. Thus, foreign trade was restricted to Guangzhou and was subject to import taxes. Naturally, this riled the European merchants and the British tried to remedy the situation by sending their first formal embassy to China, led by George Macartney, 1st Earl Macartney

(1737–1806). The delegation arrived at the Manchu court of the 83-year-old Qianlong Emperor in 1793. Unfortunately, the Chinese adopted their customary attitude towards foreigners, believing that Macartney was there to pay tribute as if from a vassal state. When he refused to *kowtow* – the elaborate, ritualistic bowing and scraping before the emperor that was expected of any visitor – there was consternation. Eventually, a compromise was reached whereby Macartney would agree to behave towards the emperor in the same way as he would if he was in the presence of his own monarch, George III. He would, therefore, kiss Qianlong's hand. The trip was wasted, however. Qianlong wrote back, dismissing British entreaties:

'The Celestial Empire possesses all things in prolific abundance and lacks no product within its borders. There is therefore no need to import the manufactures of outside barbarians in exchange for our own products.'
(*Embassy to China* by Lord Macartney, 1798, re-printed by Longmans, 1962)

This was not to be the last word, however, and soon the issue of trade would bring an end to the Middle Kingdom's splendid isolation.

Opium and 'Unequal Treaties'

There were several conflicts between China and the nations of the West in the nineteenth century, but the first and most important was the Opium War that was fought with Great Britain between 1840 and 1842. For the British, it was a symbol of their dominance of the world's oceans and its trade following the defeat of their rivals in the Napoleonic wars, but for the Chinese it came to have symbolic meaning, the bullying of the British demonstrating exactly why they considered these people to be barbarians and providing confirmation of their desire to have nothing to do with them. Opium, a derivative of the poppy, was not unfamiliar to the Chinese, having long been used for medicinal purposes. In the seventeenth century, the habit of smoking it with tobacco spread from Southeast Asia but, in the following century, the smoking of pure opium in a pipe became popular for its narcotic effects. It eased all sorts of emotional and physical pain but the major drawback was that it was addictive and withdrawal meant a great deal of pain and discomfort.

In 1729, the Yongzheng Emperor (ruled 1722–35) banned the sale of opium, a prohibition that punished dealers and the people who ran opium dens. In 1799, the drug was banned completely, a ban that remained in force until 1860. The British had originally paid for the silks, porcelain and tea that they bought from the Chinese mainly with silver, the Chinese having little interest in the luxury goods such as textiles and clocks that they tried to use. The British had by this time conquered large parts of India and they invested hugely in the manufacture of opium, realising it was a product in great demand in China that the empire did not itself produce. The British East India Company was given a monopoly over its production and export and it was shipped in chests of 60 to 65 kilos that were auctioned in Kolkata on the understanding that independent traders would smuggle it into China.

Imports of opium rose from 200 chests a year during the reign of Yongzheng to 1,000 under Qianlong, 4,000 under the Jiaqing Emperor (ruled 1796–1820) and 30,000 under his successor the Daoguang Emperor (1820–50). Disturbed by the growing dependence of his people on the drug, Daoguang took measures to stop its import and distribution. In 1838, the Chinese government official appointed to deal with the opium scourge, Lin Zexu (1785–1850), seized and destroyed 20,000 chests of opium in Guangzhou, throwing it into the sea. In the process, he apologised to the Spirit of the Sea for the pollution in a prayer that ended with the exhortation: 'tame the bestial nature of the foreigners, and make them know their God'. A chest was worth $1,000 in 1800. This represented, therefore, a substantial financial loss for the British.

Lin Zexu also wrote a moral address to Queen Victoria (ruled 1837–1901), implicating her subjects who were perpetrating a great wrong on the Chinese people, he believed, describing them as,

'...a class of treacherous barbarians who manufacture opium, smuggle it for sale and deceive our foolish people, in order to injure their bodies and derive profit therefrom. Formerly smokers were few in number, but of late the poison has spread, and its flowing poison has daily increased... Not to smoke yourselves, but yet to dare to prepare and sell to beguile the foolish masses of the Middle Kingdom – this is to protect one's own life while leading others to death, to gather profit for oneself while bringing injury upon others. Such behaviour is repugnant to the feelings of human beings, and is not tolerated by the ways of God...'

Of course, these entreaties never reached Victoria and the British, with the 'gunboat diplomacy' approach so typical of the times, declared war on China, launching what became known as the First Opium War. The very basic firearms and bows and arrows of the Qing bannermen who, in addition, had not had to take up arms for two centuries, were no match for the modern weapons of the British. The war was brought to a conclusion by the Treaty of Nanking, the first of what have become known as the Unequal Treaties imposed upon the Qing by Western states after a defeat. The Treaty of Nanking, negotiated at gunpoint, opened five Chinese ports to foreign trade – Guangzhou, Xiamen, Fuzhou, Ningbo and Shanghai. Hong Kong Island was ceded to Britain and remained in British hands until 1997 when it was handed back to the People's Republic of China. Additionally, British nationals were granted 'extra-territoriality' which made them answerable only to British law in China and the emperor had to pay an indemnity of 21 million ounces of silver to the British. Britain was also to receive 'favoured nation' status, implying that if a new privilege was extended to another nation, Britain would be granted the same privilege.

The Treaty of Nanking set the tone for the remainder of the nineteenth century during which China would be unable to set its own tariffs and, eventually, European officials would be appointed to collect duties. In 1860, the French and the English even occupied Beijing in order to enforce new treaties that increased the number of open ports by nine. Large areas within the ports were leased in perpetuity to foreign governments and these, with their inhabitants not answerable to the Chinese legal system, began to resemble international cities that were joined onto the Chinese mainland. Also as a result of these treaties, embassies and legations were established and Christian missionaries were allowed to preach across the empire.

As for opium, the situation got worse. Trade in the drug was made legal in 1860 and continued to expand for several decades. By the end of the nineteenth century, it is estimated that 10 per cent of the Chinese population – around 30 million people – were using opium and up to 50 per cent of those were addicts. Imports, however, were in decline due to the rapid increase in domestic production of the drug.

Taiping Rebellion

The import of opium increased after the treaty but so, too, did the import of European and American manufactured goods, especially textiles of which China began to import more than she exported. The impact on the people of the empire was immeasurable. Weavers and other craftsmen faced ruin while countless numbers of porters and boatmen lost their livelihoods because the inland transport system that for centuries had carried goods to and from Guangdong was rendered redundant. To pay for these imports took silver and, added to that, was the indemnity that the empire owed to the British. As the price of silver increased, the tax burden to pay for it fell, as usual, on the peasants. To make matters worse, there were famines as a result of neglect of proper irrigation and corruption amongst officials became rife.

During the 1840s there was a series of peasant revolts culminating in the biggest uprising in Chinese history, the Taiping Rebellion, which was one the world's bloodiest conflicts and certainly the largest ever civil war in terms of victims. There were risings all across China, but the main thrust was provided by the Taiping Tianguo (the Heavenly Kingdom of Great Peace), a movement that had been launched in the southeast, around Guangdong. The movement's founder was a Christian village schoolmaster named Hong Xiuquan (1814–64) who had failed the Imperial Examination four times, mainly because he could not afford to pay the requisite bribe. Consequently, he loathed the Qing ruling elite. Hong came to believe, through a series of visions, that heaven could be moved to earth by building a state consisting of people who were free and equal. This state he named the Heavenly Kingdom of Great Peace. In 1843, he established the 'Godworshipping Society' whose members tolerated no other god but the Christian one. Their intolerance of Buddhism and Daoism led to the destruction of many temples of these two religions.

The Taiping Rebellion had more fundamental objectives than previous revolts in China which had mainly attempted to overthrow the prevailing dynasty. The Taipings were advocating a radical change in Chinese society that involved a re-distribution of land that would give every peasant enough to support him and his family. It was a simple philosophy but one to which the peasantry responded enthusiastically and, in 1851, after a series of famines in the south and despite the fact that local government forces outnumbered them ten to one, they launched their revolution. From 20,000, the Taiping force rapidly increased to more than a million and, at the beginning of 1853, they seized the city of Wuhan at the intersection of the middle reaches of the Yangtze and the Han rivers in Hubei province. By spring, they had taken Nanjing where Hong established the Taiping Heavenly Kingdom's capital. They were now in control of large parts of southern China and would rule around 30 million people for eleven years under Hong.

During this period, the Taiping regime instituted a radical reform programme. They introduced flood and famine relief; institutions to provide help and care for the blind and the deaf; the banning of infanticide, still common in China; the abolition of all cruel and unjust punishment, such as the punishment of an entire family when a member did wrong; the banning of slavery and also of concubinage. The opium trade was banned and corruption was sought out and severely punished. Above all, everyone was treated equally, even women. Slavery, prostitution and the practice of footbinding were proscribed and civil service exams were opened to men and women alike. There were even units of women in the Taiping military force. Trade was suppressed and property was taken into common ownership. Most agreeable to all was the fact that the tax burden was considerably lighter than under the Qing. The Taipings saw off an attack on Nanjing by the Qing army in 1860 and widespread loathing for the Manchu rulers of the Qing maintained support for them from the peasants and artisans.

Second Opium War

Meanwhile, throughout the 1850s, the Western nations continued with their imperialist quest to carve up China between them just as they were soon to do in Africa. Furthermore, they had been demanding a revision of the treaties that had been signed following the first war over opium, revisions that would, of course, be to their advantage. Between 1856 and 1860, the Second Opium War pitted the British and the Second French Empire against China, the French becoming involved following the execution of a French missionary in Guangxi province.

On 8 October 1856, Qing water police boarded a Chinese-owned vessel, the *Arrow*, in Guangdong. Its twelve Chinese crew-members were arrested and charged with piracy and smuggling. The British demanded their release as the ship was registered in Hong Kong which was under British ownership. Even though the men were released, the British still launched an attack on Guangdong which fell without much resistance. Anglo-French forces landed at Tianjin (formerly Tientsin), close to Beijing, capturing the Taku forts.

Already engaged in fighting the Taiping rebellion, the Manchu were unable to put up much resistance and capitulated. The Treaties of Tientsin that were signed at the end of this first part of the war gave Britain, France, Russia and the United States the right to establish legations in Beijing, at the time a closed city; opened another ten ports to foreign trade; permitted all foreign vessels to navigate freely on the Yangtze; gave all foreigners the right to travel freely in China's interior which had until then been prohibited and forced China to pay large indemnities in silver to Britain and France.

A second phase of the conflict erupted when the British and French sent their envoys to Beijing and the Chinese refused to allow armed troops to conduct them to the capital. Fighting broke out again and a larger force was sent in the summer of 1860. In September that year the Qing army was annihilated at the Battle of Palikao. The Anglo-French force entered Beijing and burned the summer palaces, the Xianfeng Emperor (ruled 1850–61) having fled.

The Treaty of Tianjin and the Convention of Peking that ended the Second Opium War gave Kowloon – an area next to Hong Kong – to Britain, legalised the opium trade and granted Christians full civil rights. Importantly, foreign powers were given the right to carry Chinese workers to labour in their own lands and colonies. This launched the 'coolie' trade and Chinese workers were conveyed to work in plantations and mines in places such as Malaya, while in America they famously built the railroads. People became another exported item to be added to silk and tea. Importantly for the Manchus, however, the Western powers, concerned at the hardline Taiping stance against opium, agreed to supply them with up-to-date weaponry and to train and even lead their troops. One such leader of what was called the 'Ever Victorious Army' was an English officer by the name of Charles George Gordon (1833–85), later to become famous as General Gordon of Khartoum.

The Taipings attempted to capture Shanghai in August 1864 but were repulsed by the Qing army. From that moment on, the government forces began to re-conquer the parts of southern China they had lost and by late 1864 this had largely been achieved. Hong died of food poisoning that year and, a few days after his death, the Qing army seized Nanjing, the Taiping capital. Within five years, the last of the rebels had been defeated and the rebellion was over. It is estimated that during the fifteen years of the conflict around 20 to 30 million soldiers and civilians lost their lives, mostly to famine but many in battle. Worst of all, for the peasants, life just got harder. The foreign indemnities merely added to the tax burden and the tidal wave of western products through the many open ports destroyed countless livelihoods. The Manchus were hated even more but little could be done about them as they now had a modern, well-equipped army. Great landowners and officials had mustered their own forces against the Taipings and they retained them to counter the many small rebellions by national minorities that followed in border regions in the north and the south during the next few decades.

From 1861 to 1908, the Qing Dynasty was effectively controlled by a powerful and charismatic woman, the Empress Dowager Cixi (regency 1861–1908). She was selected to be an imperial concubine as a teenager and gave birth to a son who became the Tongzhi Emperor (ruled 1861–75) following the death of his father, Xianfeng. With Xianfeng's consort, 25-year-old Empress Dowager Ci'an (regency 1861–81), she ousted the eight regents appointed by the dying emperor to rule until the 5-year-old Tongzhi attained his majority. The two women controlled the affairs of state for twenty years together, ruling 'from behind the curtain' as it was termed – giving advice to the emperor unseen, hidden by a curtain during audiences. Following the death of Dowager Empress Ci'an, Cixi continued to wield power in the Forbidden City.

Attempts to Modernise

In 1860, with the British in the capital, the Taipings in Nanjing and the Russians making inroads into Chinese territory in Central Asia, officials feared that the Qing Dynasty was in danger of imminent collapse. Steps had to be taken to prevent this. The period between 1861 and 1865 saw the emergence of the Self-Strengthening Movement, a period of institutional reforms that attempted to modernise the empire.

Government officials firstly tried to improve the economy by making expenditure cuts as well as making strenuous efforts to repair the damaged infrastructure of the empire. Peasants were given incentives to return to their land. The army needed to be re-organised in accordance with the successful western model and the foreign powers had to be handled on their own terms, following diplomatic protocol. Factories and shipyards were built in order to manufacture the weaponry and build the ships needed to make China a modern nation. It would never be enough, however, and only served to create dissent amongst those who did not favour such attempts at modernisation or who believed it was humiliating to try to copy the foreigners.

Gradually, however, the modern world was coming to the Middle Kingdom. Newspapers published in Shanghai and Hong Kong brought coverage of international affairs and foreign travel also helped. China established legations in a number of foreign capitals including London, Paris, Madrid, Washington, Berlin and St. Petersburg. Several men became prominent in the efforts to bring China up to date, especially those known as the 'Four Famous Officials of the Late Qing'. These were Zeng Guofan (1811–72), Zuo Zongtang (1812–85), Zhang Zhidong (1837–1909) and Li Hongzhang (1823–1901). Li, for instance, was responsible for the establishment of many projects, including the setting up of the China Merchants' Steam Navigation Company, a telegraph network, the coal mines and China's first railway, linking the coal mines to the docks at Tianjin which he helped to turn into a major manufacturing centre. Such ventures were partnerships between government and private enterprise. As ever, however, bureaucratic restrictions prevented reinvestment of profits and China failed to become an industrial power to match those in the West. Other factors were also at play. The treaties the emperor had been forced to sign had opened up China to foreign manufacturers who were already established and far ahead of their indigenous rivals. In addition, there was resistance throughout the empire to the creation of a modern infrastructure of railways and telegraph and, by 1894, only 195 miles of railway track had been laid. Local resistance arose because of the belief that modern technology would create unemployment and even that it would disturb the graves of ancestors. There was also the fear – understandable, after all that had gone before – that the economic benefits brought by a modern infrastructure would remain with the ruling elite and be of no benefit to the ordinary Chinese peasant.

A Century of Change

In 1800, the population of China was 300 million, but in the course of the next fifty years that would increase by a staggering 50 million.

This, of course, brought numerous problems and the rebellions that were to follow were very much a direct result of these. Efforts were made to deal with the increased number of mouths that had to be fed. Irrigation was improved and there was a greater use of fertilisers. New crops, such as sweet potato and maize, were introduced and lands previously thought unfit for agriculture were brought into production. Deforestation to create land that could be farmed led to soil erosion and flooding, however.

Peasant families, working their farms unprofitably, increasingly sent their menfolk out to work and the women frequently wove or spun at home. The downside to this was that it was cheaper for women to spin and work from home than to have them work in an urban factory. The growth of textile factories was, therefore, inhibited because they were unable to compete. Feuds over land, water and tenancy rights became common and the trying financial situation of many families led to an increase in female infanticide. Parents wanted sons who could work more profitably. This, in turn, led to fewer marriageable women and the removal of the need for young men to stay home and bring up a family. They tended to drift towards urban centres where they found work. Meanwhile, as the price of opium rose inexorably, China's economy entered an extended period of deflation and recession. The arrival of manufacturing brought immense changes. In 1875, just about all China's cotton yarn was spun by hand. By 1905 only half was hand-spun. Thousands of village families that had brought in extra income from women hand-spinning at home suffered as a result.

Like the Europeans, many Chinese saw emigration as a way to make the most of the opportunities the world had to offer. Chinese from the southern coastal areas of Fujian and Guangdong had moved throughout Southeast Asia since Ming times, in search of trading wealth. In many of those places, distinct Chinese communities existed and local authorities were often happy to let them administrate their own areas. European exploitation of places like Singapore also opened the door for entrepreneurial Chinese who flooded on to that island after it was founded in 1819. Chinese from Guangdong worked in the tin mines of Malaysia and, in Kuala

Lumpur and Singapore, the Chinese became the dominant ethnic group. By 1900, more than half a million Chinese were living in the Dutch East Indies (present-day Indonesia).

Following the banning of the African slave trade, labour contractors increasingly turned to China for workers. Hundreds of thousands of Chinese labourers – known as 'coolies' – signed up to work in the plantations of places such as Cuba, Peru, Hawaii and Sumatra. The slave trade might have ended, but the Chinese – promised easy money – were treated little better than slaves. There was voluntary migration, too. The discovery of gold in California in 1848, Australia in 1851 and British Columbia in 1858 drew many Chinese and a few did, indeed, strike it rich. Others went on to find work building America's railroads while some became miners. Nonetheless, there was friction between the Chinese and other Americans and they were prohibited from becoming American citizens in 1882. Immigration was also stopped, often making it impossible for a Chinese labourer to bring his wife and children to America.

As China faltered in its efforts to transform itself into a modern industrial nation, the Japanese moved ahead. They had succeeded on a number of fronts; Japan had a constitutional monarchy, a universal education system, a modern military and new industries. Japan was also making inroads on China's influence in Southeast Asia. The two countries came to blows in 1894 when rebellion broke out in Korea, one of Qing China's most loyal tributary states. China lost the ensuing war badly and had to agree to cede to the Japanese the island of Taiwan as well as pay a huge indemnity to the victor. This heavy defeat was all the West needed to start believing that China was in no state to defend its empire effectively. As they had done in Africa, they began to take concessions. In 1898, Russia signed a 25-year lease on the Liaodong Peninsula and established a naval base at Port Arthur. Meanwhile, France, Germany and Britain secured even more port and trade concessions. Germany acquired Jiaozhou, France took Guangzhouwan and the British leased Weihai.

Hundred Days' Reform and the Boxer Rebellion

The Tongzhi Emperor died suddenly of smallpox in 1875, having ruled for fourteen years, but it was a rule over which his mother, Dowager Empress Cixi, had cast a long shadow. Cixi flouted the laws of succession by installing her 4-year-old nephew, ruling as the Guangxu Emperor (ruled 1875–1908), although, needless to say, she would remain the real power in the empire until her death in 1908, playing her ministers against each other masterfully in order to maintain her position.

Cixi, known as the 'Old Buddha', was a daunting character, a five-feet-tall, heavily made-up fireball who, like other Manchu women, wore her fingernails long. She used them to scratch the faces of servant girls who did not meet her high standards. She would fly into a rage if criticised and was not open to bad news. She was of dubious morality, partial to young officers, and she spent extravagantly on the Forbidden City and the Summer Palace. Money that had been put to one side for modernising the out-of-date Chinese navy was spent by her on building a marble boat on a lake at the Summer Palace.

By 1898, China was in a parlous state, at the mercy of the West and with internal threats simmering. At this point Guangxu, more reform-minded than the ultra-conservative Dowager Empress, threw his support behind a group of reformers led by political thinker, Kang Youwei (1858–1927), and launched what has become known as the Hundred Days' Reform, a radical, national, cultural, political and educational reform movement. Based on the examples of Japan and Russia, it had a number of objectives: to modernise the exam system; to eliminate sinecures; to create a modern education system; to introduce democracy and make China a constitutional monarchy; to strengthen the economy using the ideas of capitalism; to strengthen and modernise the military and to industrialise the empire. The movement lasted only 104 days – from 11 June to 21 September – before Cixi and her supporters crushed it.

Guanxu never recovered from the disappointment of this failure and remained a virtual prisoner for the remainder of his life, Cixi even bricking up the windows of his chambers in the Summer Palace. In order to curry favour with the West, however, she could not afford to dethrone him. The only alternative for her was to get rid of the westerners and to achieve this she threw her considerable support behind the growing nationalist group, the Righteous Harmony Society, who created the Boxer Rebellion between 1898 and 1901, opposing foreign imperialism and Christianity in China. In 1900, Cixi abandoned the long-held policy of suppressing the Boxers, a decision that brought protests from the West. The movement spread north from Shandong to close to Beijing, its members burning churches, murdering Chinese Christians and intimidating Chinese officials who tried to stop them. The Western powers sent troops to guard their legations in Beijing that were by this time besieged. Disguised as a peasant, the emperor fled the capital for Xi'an in a cart.

After the siege had been lifted by the foreign troops, an international expeditionary force under the command of German General Alfred Graf von Waldersee (1832–1904) occupied Beijing, Tianjin and other northern cities for more than a year. The Summer Palace was sacked and there was what the media described as 'an orgy of looting'. Needless to say, the West imposed a heavy penalty on the Chinese. An astonishing indemnity of 450 million ounces of silver, worth around $330 million, was to be deducted from customs and salt revenues during the ensuing forty years. The westerners were also given the right to fortify and defend Beijing's legation quarter. China was effectively under the protection of foreign powers. The empire's economy was in ruins – imports far exceeded exports and the development of industry and the railways was in the hands of foreign entrepreneurs. Furthermore, the major ports were controlled by the nations of the West. As the debt mounted, the situation in the Middle Kingdom could not have been worse.

The Manchus were thoroughly discredited, leading to threats to their continuity from every direction. Mandarins and regional governors had established powerful forces under their own command, supporting them through a new tax, the *likin*, a duty imposed on inland trade. Heavy taxation further alienated businessmen and traders from the Manchus and peasants across the empire formed secret anti-Manchu societies.

Returning to the capital in 1902, Cixi and her ministers began to introduce reforms that approximated to those of 1898. Education was modernised, thousands of schools were opened and a modern police force was established. The army was reorganised and military academies were opened. The traditional examination system, based on the classics, was abolished, a bitter pill for the conservative scholar-gentry to swallow. However, she failed to announce reform of the Chinese financial system or the elimination of corruption.

In 1908, Cixi announced a plan for reform that would lead to the creation of a constitutional monarchy in nine years. Before it could begin, however, the Empress Dowager died, aged 73. Following her death, it was announced that Emperor Guangxu had passed away the previous day. In 2008, forensic tests established that he had died of acute arsenic poisoning. It has been speculated that Cixi, close to death, had her nephew murdered to prevent him introducing even more radical reforms when she was gone. The formidable Dowager Empress Cixi had even tried to control China from beyond the grave.

6. Prelude to Revolution

The First Republic (1912 to 1949)

The nineteenth century had been disastrous for China and the Qing Dynasty would come to an ignominious end not long after the start of the new one. The West had embraced dramatic change during the Qing era – from the Renaissance to the Age of Discovery, the Reformation, the Enlightenment, the French Revolution and the Industrial Revolution. China, on the other hand, had stagnated, throwing away the advantages it had once held in science, technology and transportation. The world had moved on, leaving China not only behind but also at its mercy.

Who was responsible for this state of affairs? Some of the principal culprits were the Manchu officials who resented and prevented every attempt to learn from the West, inhibiting any progress that China might make. Those who believed that government sponsorship of industrial and infrastructure projects would work, eschewing the benefits that capitalism brought to Western industry, must also take some of the blame. Even the rebellions that broke out sporadically throughout the century were inadequate, lacking the vision and leadership that might have made a difference.

The credibility and moral authority of the Qing had been seriously weakened. This gave rise to the emergence in regions across the empire of activists who were determined to reconstruct China's political order. It would be a painful process, a struggle between warlords, Nationalists, Communists, idealists and opportunists but it would bring to an end China's 2,000-year-old tradition of monarchical rule.

The last emperor was named by the dying Cixi as her three-year-old great-nephew, Puyi, the Xuantong Emperor (ruled 1908–12). Due to the youth of the boy-emperor, power passed to a group of arrogant Manchu princes with Puyi's father, Prince Chun (1883–1951), as regent. As the ruling elite toyed with notions of reform, many Chinese were studying and preparing for change, not change brought about by the government, however; change introduced by them.

The best-known reformers of the first decade of the twentieth century were probably Kang Youwei, who had travelled widely after falling foul of Dowager Empress Cixi during the Hundred Days' Reform in 1898, and Liang Qichao (1873–1929) who settled in Japan where, by 1906, more than 10,000 passionately nationalist Chinese students were studying. Liang encouraged their 'dangerous thoughts' by publishing magazines that criticised China and promoted democracy and the adoption of western ideas.

In 1905, several revolutionary groups merged to form one organisation – the Tongmenghui (Revolutionary Alliance) – with a programme made up of what they termed the 'Three People's Principles'. These were Nationalism – the freeing of China from the foreign yoke; Democracy – the overthrow of the Manchu Dynasty and the introduction to China of a democratic republic; the People's Livelihood – the re-distribution of land so that each family would have the means to be self-sufficient. The founder and leader of this movement was Sun Zhongshan (1866–1925) who became better known as Sun Yatsen. Sun was from Guangdong, born of peasant stock in a region that had been a Taiping stronghold. In 1878, when he was thirteen, he travelled to Hawaii where his elder brother had settled, but in 1883, with his brother afraid that Sun Yatsen would become a Christian, he was sent home. He was later baptised in Hong Kong where he was studying western medicine. It was during this time that he and his friends began to formulate their political thinking, making plans for China to become a republic.

In 1894, Sun returned to Hawaii where he founded the Revive China Society which was committed to revolution. When Revive China merged with the Furen Literary Society, another revolutionary organisation, he became secretary with the FLS's Yeung Kui-wan (1861–1901) taking the role of president. They were based in Hong Kong. Following the Sino-Japanese War of 1895, the organisation split into two factions, Yeung and others advocating the Hundred Days' Reform, Sun and his group demanding nothing short of the replacement of the dynastic system by a modern republic.

On 26 October 1895, Revive China plotted the First Guangzhou Uprising. Sun Yatsen and others planned to seize Guangzhou but their plans were leaked to the Qing government. Seventy members were arrested and many were executed. Pressured by the Chinese government, the Hong Kong government barred Sun Yatsen and Yeung Kai-wan from entering the territory for five years. Yeung Kai-wan was assassinated by Qing agents in Hong Kong in 1901 while Sun Yatsen visited Japan, America, Canada and Great Britain, continuing his studies, developing his thinking and raising funds for his movement. In 1896, he was kidnapped in London by the staff of the Chinese legation and would have been smuggled back to China for trial and almost certain execution had he not managed to secrete in a laundry basket a note asking for help to a former teacher. The man went to the police and secured Sun's release.

Other important revolutionary figures of the time included Zou Rong (1885–1905) who wrote a pamphlet highly critical of what he described as 'the maladministration of the ambitious, tribal, rapacious Manchus'. He claimed that the Manchus' treatment of the Chinese provided complete justification for revolution. He was tried and imprisoned, dying before the end of his sentence. Qiu Jin (1875–1907) was a well-educated woman from a gentry family. In 1903, convinced that China was on the road to disaster, she unbound her feet, left her husband and travelled to Japan to study. She became famous for dressing in male clothing, carrying a short sword and arguing with other Chinese students whom she accused of showing apathy. She returned to China to teach, but plotted revolution with the anti-Qing Restoration Society. When their plot was discovered, Qiu made no attempt to escape. She was arrested, refused to give in under torture and was executed.

The Revolutionary Alliance sponsored a number of attempted

rebellions during the next few years while Sun travelled, raising funds and soliciting foreign supporters. It was while he was thus engaged that the collapse of Chinese imperial rule began. Meanwhile, the government moved slowly towards reform. In 1909, consultative provincial assemblies met in each province and representatives of each were sent to Beijing. These were elected and, although very few were permitted to vote, there was still excitement about this initial taste of participatory government. Soon, however, it was forgotten in the heat of revolution.

The Xinhai Revolution was known thus because it erupted in 1911, the year of the Xinhai stem-branch in the cycle of the Chinese calendar. While Sun was in Denver in the United States, a bomb exploded in the headquarters of the revolutionary group in Wuchang, the capital of Hubei province. The revolutionaries seized the city and telegraphed other provinces encouraging them also to declare independence. Fifteen provinces had done so within six weeks. The government sent General Yuan Shikai (1859–1916) to negotiate with the rebels. He had attained a position of political importance after being responsible for the training of China's first modern army. By 1912, he was virtually running the country, and had forced Prince Chun to resign his regency. The rebels, fearful of intervention on the emperor's behalf by other states, reached a compromise with Yuan. The emperor would abdicate and General Yuan would become president of a Chinese republic.

On 29 December 1911, a meeting of provincial representatives in Nanking had elected Sun Yatsen 'provisional president' of the Republic of China. A Provisional Government had assembled, a republican calendar system, with 1912 as the first year, had been introduced, as well as the new Zhongshan suit (later known as the 'Mao Suit'). This new fashion style was a deliberate attempt to distance the wearer from the Manchu style of dress that the Qing Dynasty had imposed on Chinese as well as to create a simple style that symbolised proletarian unity. As the influence of the West grew in China during the 1990s, this style of clothing became rare on the streets of China, but Chinese leaders still wear the Zhongshan at important events.

Yuan Shikai, meanwhile, was in command of the Beiyang Army, northern China's military force and the most powerful army in China. Believing that General Yuan was probably the only man who could preserve China's national unity, Sun Yatsen agreed to step down as president if Yuan organised the abdication of Puyi and the end of Manchu rule. In February 1912, the last Qing emperor abdicated, ending 2,000 years of imperial rule in China. In accordance with an agreement signed with the new Republic of China, Puyi was to retain his imperial title and would be treated by the new government with the protocol conferred on a foreign monarch. He and his retinue were to be permitted to continue to live in the northern half of the Forbidden City, in their private apartments, and would also have use of the Summer Palace. He was granted a substantial annual payment by the Republic although this was never paid in full and was stopped altogether after just a few years.

The Early Republic: 1912–28

Following the abdication of Puyi, Sun Yatsen accordingly resigned and Yuan became president on 10 March 1912, his efforts to establish a republic funded by a group of foreign bankers. A republican constitution was proclaimed and, in August 1912, China's first elections for a Senate and a House of Representatives were called. Only about five per cent of the population qualified to vote, however. The Tongmenhui merged with four other parties in order to give nationalists a chance to win some power, calling themselves the Kuomintang (the Nationalist Party) and Song Jiaoren (1882–1913) took the role of leader. The Kuomintang won a majority of seats in both houses and Song used this new power to severely criticise Yuan's government for its borrowing from Western powers and its lack of progress on the question of Outer Mongolia which had declared independence and accepted the protection of Russia. Song became too great a problem for Yuan and, on 20 March 1913, government agents shot him dead in a Shanghai railway station.

Animosity towards Yuan grew, especially as he began to make important decisions without consulting parliament, behaving increasingly like a military dictator. One such decision was to accept the 'Reorganisation Loan', a loan of £25 million by a consortium of British, French and German financiers, ostensibly to reorganise China's administrative system but believed by many to be a fund to be used in the suppression of government opposition. In July 1913, after Yuan had moved against the military governors of the provinces of south and central China, the Second Revolution took place after six provinces declared independence from the new republic. The Kuomintang's military force was defeated by Yuan's army on 1 August and the rebellion was soon suppressed. Sun Yatsen and other rebels fled to Japan. In October, Yuan was formally elected President of the Republic of China and, after agreeing to provide autonomy to Tibet and Outer Mongolia, the new nation received formal recognition by the major powers. This gave Yuan the chance to launch a campaign of violent repression. He declared martial law, shutting down newspapers and arresting and executing thousands, 22,000 people dying in Henan province alone.

He also launched an attack on the constitution, and, by 1914, it had been amended to make him President for Life and to make his position hereditary. He expelled Kuomintang members of parliament and dissolved the party. By the middle of 1915, he had control of twelve of China's eighteen provinces and his power was growing in the other six. Meanwhile, momentous events were gathering speed in Europe.

The Twenty One Demands and Imperial Aspirations

When the First World War broke out, China was at first neutral. Japan, on the other hand, sided with the Allies against Germany and Austria-Hungary. The Japanese seized the opportunity to capture German concessions in China but there was little doubt that they also saw it as an opportunity to seize control of the whole country. This desperate situation provided Yuan with an opportunity to demonstrate why he was the best person to lead the country. He had argued, after all, that the only way to stop foreign powers from encroaching on the Middle Kingdom was through national unity. However, Japan's successes in the First Sino-Japanese War of 1895 and the Russo-Japanese War of 1904–5 had persuaded her leaders that they, like the European imperialist powers, had a chance to establish economic domination of China and gain easy access to its markets as well as its raw materials.

On 18 January 1915, Japanese Prime Minister Okuma Shigenobu (1838–1922) and Foreign Minister Kato Takaaki (1860–1926) sent Yuan Shikai a set of twenty-one demands with a warning of dire consequences should they be turned down. The demands amounted to the total subjugation of China, including amongst other things: the transfer of Germany's former 'rights' in China to Japan and control of the Manchurian railways and ports; the insistence that no Chinese port should be leased to any other power than Japan; and that Chinese iron and steel works, mines and arsenals be run jointly by the Japanese and the Chinese. They further demanded that the police should be placed under Sino-Japanese control. Japanese 'advisers' were to be involved in every sphere of government as well as in military matters. For Yuan, it was a matter of gaining Japanese support for his imperial ambitions and, in May 1915, he agreed to many of the main demands although he did not concede to those concerning advisers. That would have made China little more than a Japanese dependency.

In November 1915, a specially convened assembly voted unanimously in favour of President Yuan becoming emperor and, on 12 December, Yuan accepted, declaring that he would become emperor, under the era name of Hongxian, on the first day of the following year. Opposition to this move was swift and decisive and on 25 December the province of Yunnan, led by the military leader and warlord, Cai E (1882–1916), declared independence, launching the National Protection War. Yuan's army suffered several defeats, inspiring other southern provinces – Guizhou and Guangxi – also to declare independence. Some of Yuan's most loyal supporters, including the Beiyang Army general, Feng Guozhang (1859–1919), commander of the garrison at Nanjing, deserted him. On 22 March, Yuan formally abandoned his plan to make China a monarchy once more, but this was not enough for his enemies. On 5 June, however, as more provinces ceded from the Republic of China, Yuan solved the problem by suddenly dying of kidney failure.

The Warlord Period (1916–28)

In the twelve years following Yuan's death, political chaos reigned. The former empire was divided amongst military cliques during a period in which the Republican government in Beijing was nothing more than a gesture. Wars were waged across China, as groups of generals, each supported by one or more foreign power, slugged it out. Meanwhile, taking advantage of the chaos, bandit gangs once more stalked the countryside causing mayhem. In the north, recognition was usually given to anyone who was in control of Beijing and, even if they opposed the government in place at any one time, the various factions still recognised its legitimacy.

Former Qing general, Li Yuanhong (1864–1928), was pressed into office as president by the Beiyang Army generals after the death of Yuan Shikai and the constitution of 1912 was re-introduced. Power was in the hands, however, of his prime minister, Duan Qirui, (1865–1936) who had also occupied that position in Yuan's government. He clumsily attempted to push China into the First World War and was also secretly receiving money from the Japanese, both of which led Li to dismiss him in May 1917. To safeguard himself against action by Duan, Li solicited the support of another influential Beiyang general, Zhang Xun (1854–1923). Surprisingly, Zhang attempted to restore the monarchy in July 1917 but was thwarted by Duan who regained control. As a result of this action, when General Feng Guozhang became president of the republic on 1 August 1917, following Li Yuanhong's resignation, Duan was once again asked to be premier.

With Duan Qirui back in power, Sun Yatsen decided to establish an alternative government in Guangzhou, leading Duan to capture Hunan province and accept military advisers and loans from the Japanese. The Beiyang Army split over these issues into two factions, the Anhui – supporters of Duan – and the Zhili – initially supporters of General Feng. The Anhui clique was initially dominant but the Zhili eventually defeated it with the help of the Manchurian warlord, Zhang Zuolin (1875–1928). In 1924, probably the low-point in the Warlord Era, a further split led to the Japanese-backed

Fengtians defeating the Zhili clique in battle. Following this development, more stable regional regimes emerged – Zhang Zuolin in Manchuria and the northeast; Yan Xishan (1883–1960) in the backward province of Shanxi; Sun Chuanfang (1885–1935) in the provinces of the lower Yangtze; Wu Peifu (1874–1939) in the middle Yangtze; the Guangxi clique – a major group of warlords – in the south; and Feng Yuxiang (1882–1948) in the northwest, although his rule was less stable.

Throughout this period, meanwhile, a government recognised by foreign powers continued to operate from Beijing. It declared war on Germany and Austria-Hungary in 1917, allowing it to annul the indemnity payments due to those countries as well as their extraterritorial rights. At the Washington Conference of 1921–22, Japan agreed to withdraw from Shandong and Britain gave up her lease on Weihai.

At the end of the Warlord Era, the Chinese revolution had become mired in confusion. The civil service had collapsed, the scholar class was no longer involved in government and the rich had abandoned the dangers of living in a countryside where bandits and armies roamed and did as they wished. The highly effective irrigation and drainage projects that had helped farmers fell into disrepair and floods and famines ensued. Nonetheless, it can be argued that, without a strong central government wielding its authority over the lives and thoughts of its people, China was host to an unheard-of degree of intellectual freedom that would result in the next stage of the revolution.

The Beginnings of the Chinese Communist Party

The extraordinary intellectual revolution that China underwent between 1917 and 1921 is encapsulated by the term the May Fourth Movement, sometimes called the New Culture Movement. It is often described as the starting point of modern Chinese history and had amongst its members a number of the people who would shape China's future, including Mao Zedong (1893–1976), founding father of the People's Republic of China.

It began with nationalist agitation on 4 May 1919, when 3,000 students demonstrated in Beijing in protest at the decision made by the Paris Peace Conference to transfer Germany's interests in China to Japan. Soon, the action had become a national protest. Japanese goods were boycotted and hundreds of other cities joined in. It was a movement supported by a broad cross-section of the Chinese people, anxious to preserve Chinese integrity and, in the case of merchants embracing the nationalist cause, safeguarding markets against foreign intervention. It brought strong criticism of the past, particularly of Confucianism – most notably in the magazine *Xinqingniang* (also known as *New Youth* or *La Jeunesse*), founded by Chen Duxiu (1879–1942). It viewed the West as the solution to the problems China was facing.

Culturally, too, there was a revolution, the vernacular – *baihua*– replacing the classical form – *wenyan* – in literary works by such writers as Lu Xun (1881–1936). In 1920, the education ministry ordered that *baihua* be used in textbooks instead of *wenyan*. Such changes emerged from an intelligentsia, estimated to have numbered around 5 million, that had been educated in Western-style schools and from a bourgeoisie that had become politically powerful. As the protests continued, the Beijing government resigned while its delegation to the peace conference in Paris, reacting to pressure from the protests, refused to endorse the Versailles Treaty.

The founding of the Chinese Communist Party (CCP) began around 1920, by which time there were a number of converts to Marxism, usually living near universities. Amongst these early converts were Chen Duxiu, founder of *Xinqingniang* and Li Dazhao (1888–1927) at Beijing University as well as 27-year-old Mao Zedong in Changsha, capital of Hunan in south-central China. In July 1921, 53 men attended the First Congress of the CCP that took place in Shanghai and then Jiaxing at which the name *Zhongguo Gongchan Dang* (Chinese Communist Party) was formally adopted. Chen Duxiu was appointed secretary but other key attendees were Li Dazhao, Chen Gongbo (1892–1946), Zhang Guotao (1897–1979), Dong Biwu (1886–1975), Li Da ((1890–1966), Chen Tanqiu (1896–1943), Zhou Fohai (1897–1948), He Shuheng (1876–1935) and Mao Zedong. Work began on establishing labour centres and workers' schools and Mao was busy with the Hunan labour movement as well as the organisation of four strikes between 1920 and 1923.

Meanwhile, Sun Yatsen was back in Guangzhou but his Kuomintang's membership was now only a few thousand. In 1923, the Kuomintang allied itself with the CCP with the common aim of getting rid of foreign powers and unifying China. The Kuomintang then underwent reorganisation along Leninist lines under the tutelage of the fledgling Soviet Union, with Soviet military advisers and funding. A military academy was opened at Huangpu, south of Guangzhong. In March 1925, the Nationalist cause was dealt a severe blow when Sun Yatsen died of cancer before he could send an expedition north to defeat the warlords and unify China. His position as leader of the KMT was taken by his close ally, Chiang-Kai-Shek (1887–1975).

Born in Xikou, near Ningbo in the southeastern coastal province of Zheijiang, Chiang received military training in Tokyo, where he first met Sun Yatsen. In 1908, he joined the KMT's precursor, the Tongmenghui. After serving in the Imperial Japanese Army for two years, he returned to China in 1911, joining the revolutionary forces. During the rule of Yuan Shikai, he divided his time between the International Settlement in Shanghai and Japan. In 1915, he took part in the murder of the leader of the Restoration Society and a year later became leader of the Chinese Revolutionary Party. In early 1924, Sun sent Chiang to Moscow for three months to study the Soviet military and political system and during the trip he met Leon Trotsky and other Soviet leaders. He quickly realised, however, that the Soviet model would not work in China. Prior to taking over as leader, he was in command of the KMT's Whampoa Military Academy.

British soldiers shot dead twelve protesting students in Shanghai on 30 May 1925, leading to an eruption of national feeling that dwarfed the May Fourth Movement protests. Strikes and further deaths at the hands of British and French troops helped to rapidly increase membership of both the Kuomintang and the CCP. A campaign in the east by the National Revolutionary Army (NRA) – the military wing of the KMT – had brought much of Guangdong province under its control. Further action was necessary, it was concluded, to bring about the final reunification of China.

The Northern Expedition

The Northern Expedition by the NRA, led by Chiang Kai-shek, began in July 1926, the CCP organising the peasants and workers in the areas through which the army would pass. Nonetheless, there were grave differences between the KMT and the CCP. Chiang had always opposed Sun's policy of alliance with the Soviet Union and the CCP, and the KMT were against the class warfare espoused by the Communists. Many in the KMT army were staunchly anti-communist. In April 1927, Chiang instigated a purge of Chinese Communist Party members in Shanghai, known as the 'White Terror', in which around 12,000 died. Such action was also carried out by Kuomintang members across China during the next year and at least 300,000 communists and dissidents are estimated to have lost their lives. By the end of that year, not only was Chiang undisputed leader of the Nationalists, his army had also gained control of the seven provinces of south and central China. Chiang transferred the Kuomintang government from Guangzhou to Wuhan.

There were Kuomintang elements – led by Wang Jingwei (1883–1944) – who disagreed with Chiang's purge, leading to a factional split in his organisation. Chiang established his own capital at Nanjing while his opponents remained at Wuhan. The result was a weakened Kuomintang through the summer of 1927 and the strengthening of the warlords' armies to the north. Chiang now repudiated the alliance with the Soviet Union and the communists and made membership of the CCP a capital crime. In the autumn of 1927, the Wuhan government gave in to pressure and reconciled itself with Chiang in Nanjing. In April 1928, the Nationalists swept away the remnants of the warlord armies, reaching the Yellow River. On 4 June, the Nationalist Army took Beijing – re-named 'Beiping' (Northern Peace) – but Chiang retained Nanjing as capital. No matter where the capital was, however, China was once again unified as one state under the dictatorship of Chiang Kai-shek and was recognised as such by the western powers.

The Nanjing Decade: 1928–37

The Kuomintang now ruled all of the former Chinese Empire, apart from Mongolia, Tibet, Xinjiang and Manchuria. From 1928 until 1937, from the victorious conclusion of the Northern Expedition to the outbreak of war with Japan, they ruled from their capital, Nanjing. Many returned students were appointed to key government posts and, over the next few years, China began to reclaim control of her own affairs, reducing the number of foreign concessions from thirty-three to thirteen and regaining control of such things as customs tariffs, Salt Administration and the Post Office.

A military man, Chiang turned his attention to the modernisation of his army. Advisers from Nazi Germany helped him plan his campaigns against the communists at their base in Jianxi. China also received arms shipments from Germany. Western economists, meanwhile, undertook the overhaul of the Chinese financial system and engineers from the West helped to update China's outmoded and neglected transport and communications networks. In his first few years in power, Chiang borrowed ideas from the emerging fascist regimes in Europe, launching in 1934 the New Life Movement. Its goal was to 'militarise the life of the people of the entire nation... to make them willing to sacrifice for the nation at all times'. Adherents were named 'Blueshirts' and would become Chiang's hated secret police.

China was undergoing dramatic change. In the streets many people – mainly of the middle class – could be seen in western dress and even architectural styles changed. No longer were buildings hidden behind walls as in the past. They now took on a more European design and aspect. Those who had studied abroad brought back technical expertise in many fields. The changes, however, were taking place mainly in the cities. For the rural peasant, little had changed since Qing times. He was still beset by problems of deforestation, flooding, soil erosion and exhaustion and, as ever, high rents and exploitation. The increase in population – there were 500 million Chinese in 1930 – did nothing to help the situation, merely putting more pressure on available land. The Depression in Europe and America was also hurting exports of silk and tea. Meanwhile, the Nationalist government did little to help.

Women had already been experiencing change at the start of the twentieth century. Footbinding, for instance – the practice of painfully binding the feet of young girls to restrict growth – which had probably originated amongst court dancers in the early Song Dynasty – had become a source of embarrassment for China as foreigners highlighted its barbarity. Anti-footbinding societies emerged in the 1890s and the practice began to diminish as the twentieth century wore on, until after 1930 it was only to be found in remote, underdeveloped areas. Schools for women had become increasingly common and, by 1919, there were 134,000 girls' schools with more than 4.5 million students. The Nationalists drafted a new civil code in 1930 in which women were given the right to choose their husbands as well as to repudiate arranged marriages. They were also given almost the same rights as men regarding divorce and when they did the same work as men they were to be paid the same wage. The right to inherit property equally with their brothers was also opened to them. As before, however, little changed in the countryside where arranged marriages continued to take place.

In terms of foreign policy, there was still the threat of Japan to deal with. The Japanese retained their ambition to subjugate China while they also greedily eyed the Soviet Union's eastern provinces. To this end, they had consolidated their position in Manchuria, gained after the defeat of Tsarist Russia in 1905. In autumn 1931, they attacked the Chinese forces in Mukden in Manchuria and had soon captured the whole of that industrially developed province. China appealed to the League of Nations but, although the action was condemned, nothing was done to secure the withdrawal of Japanese troops from the region. Japan proclaimed Manchuria to be an independent state, giving it the name 'Manchukuo'. They set up a puppet regime, installing Puyi, the last Qing emperor, as Head of State and then emperor.

In 1932, the Japanese attacked Shanghai and civilian areas were bombed, actions that were roundly condemned. After four months they withdrew, but only after Chiang had signed an agreement that allowed them to station troops in the region. He believed that Japanese firepower was so superior to his own that there was little point resisting. Anyway, his main priority at that time was, as he described it, 'internal pacification before resistance to external attack'; in other words, to deal with internal enemies, the communists who had taken to the hills and were garnering the support of the peasants. It is estimated that between 1927 and 1932 a million people lost their lives in the struggle.

The communists fought back when they could, however, and a series of peasant rebellions occurred, led by men such as Mao Zedong and Zhu De (1886–1976). Mao was from a farming family in Hunan and his father was moderately wealthy. He passed through the new modern school system before training to be a teacher in Changsha. After graduation, he went to Beijing where he worked in the library of Beijing University but in his spare time attended discussion groups organised by Chinese intellectuals and Chinese Communist Party co-founder, Li Dazhao. From there he went to Hunan and was one of Hunan's representatives at the First Communist Party meeting in 1921. Following Chiang's purges, he headed for the mountains with a few thousand men. They based themselves between Jiangxi and Hunan, forming the first elements of the Chinese Red Army, later to be known as the People's Liberation Army. In the areas where they operated, the estates of rich landowners were confiscated and distributed amongst peasants and farm labourers, the tax burden was lightened and the people elected their own councils, known as 'soviets'. An American journalist described a conversation with a peasant:

'There was a peasant lad who had joined the Reds in Szechuan, and I asked him why he had done so. He told me that his parents were poor farmers, with only four *mou* of land (less than an acre), which wasn't enough to feed him and his two sisters. When the Reds came to his village he said, all the peasants welcomed them, brought them hot tea and made sweets for them. The Red dramatists gave plays. It was a happy time. Only the landlords ran. When the land was redistributed his parents received their share. So they were not sorry but very glad when he joined the "poor people's army".'

The lack of agrarian reform and famines in the late twenties and early thirties created widespread discontent and persuaded increasing numbers of peasants to enlist in the Red Army or to engage in rebellion in their region. Chiang was concerned enough to dispatch four expeditions between 1930 and 1932 to seek out communist bases. They did not fare well against the guerilla tactics of the troops commanded by Zhu and Mao. The guerrillas had four slogans that explained these:

'When the enemy advances, we retreat!
When the enemy halts and encamps, we trouble them!
When the enemy tries to avoid a battle, we attack!
When the enemy retreats, we pursue!'

At the end of 1931, the communists proclaimed a 'Chinese Soviet Republic' in Jianxi with Mao Zedong occupying the role of Chairman of the provisional government. In 1933, Chiang made a last, desperate effort to annihilate the communists, sending an army of half a million troops, supported by 400 planes. The 100,000 rifles of the Red Army were unsupported by artillery or aircraft and, after almost a year of desperate fighting, it looked at last as if Chiang was about to defeat the communists.

On 16 October 1934, completely encircled by Nationalist forces and with defeat staring them in the face, about 80,000 communist soldiers and porters launched a two-pronged attack in the south and west. Their attack worked and around 86,000 soldiers and civilians succeeded in breaking out. Behind them were left more than 20,000 wounded troops and most of the wives and children who had been with them at their base. This was the beginning of one of Communist China's greatest stories – the Long March. Under the command of Mao Zedong and Zhou Enlai (1898–1976), the communists escaped in a circling retreat to the west and north that took them 8,000 miles in over 370 days. Suffering enormous numbers of casualties, they crossed south and southwest China before turning north to Shaanxi. The march was a phenomenal feat of endurance and the communists were faced with major obstacles such as the Tatu River. Only around 8,000 of the original force made it to the end of the journey, although they were bolstered by those who joined en route, bringing their number to 20,000. They stopped and established a base at Yan'an in central Shaanxi and there they made homes by cutting caves out of the cliffs. A military academy, hospitals, a college of art and other facilities were established in the cliff grottoes. It was a venture that has been endlessly mythologised over the decades since.

However, some things were established by the march. The communists were now free of Soviet influence; they had perfected the guerrilla ethic; they had instilled in themselves infinite reserves of discipline and loyalty and they had found a leader – Mao Zedong.

The Second Sino-Japanese War

The Japanese were hated in China. They abducted women for prostitution and men were taken for forced labour projects. Their ruthless policy when faced with resistance – 'killing all, burning all, looting all' – gave the Chinese common cause against their detested enemy. There had been intermittent incidents between the two countries since 1931, the last of which was the Marco Polo Bridge Incident (also known as the Lugouqiao Incident) of 1937, a battle between the two sides fought at the Marco Polo Bridge outside the walled town of Wanping, southwest of Beijing. Another incident, perpetrated not by the Japanese, but by Zhang Xueliang (1901–2001), former warlord of Manchuria, not only brought war against the Japanese, but, according to Nationalist writers, prevented the almost inevitable defeat of the communist forces, allowing them to regroup. Chiang Kai-shek was following his policy of defeating the internal enemy before facing the external threat, a policy that disappointed many Chinese, including many Nationalists. Zhang effectively kidnapped Chiang during the leader's December 1936 visit to his base at Xi'an in order to urge him to take more effective action against the communists. He kept the leader prisoner until he agreed to end the civil war and join with his enemies to form a united front against the Japanese. When agreement had been reached, Chiang and Zhang travelled to Nanjing where Chiang immediately had Zhang arrested. He would remain a prisoner for fifty years, both in China and then, from 1949, in Taiwan. Nonetheless, an armistice was reached with the communists who agreed to place the Red Army under the command of the 'Generalissimo' as the western media had nicknamed Chiang. They also agreed to acknowledge the authority of the Nanjing government.

In July 1937, shortly after the Marco Polo Bridge Incident, Japanese troops occupied Beijing and launched bombing raids on Chinese cities. Almost a million troops were put into the field. Initial Chinese success gave way to defeats in the south and, by the end of 1937, Shanghai was in Japanese hands. Not long after, Nanjing had also fallen. In 1938, most of the coastal areas, including Guangzhou, had been taken and the Japanese were advancing up the Yangtze River towards Wuhan. Most of eastern China was now under Japanese control, leading Chiang to move his government to Chongqing in the southwest of the country. The only means of communication with it now was through Burma.

The Second World War broke out in Europe in 1939 but, when Japan attacked the United States fleet at Pearl Harbor in December 1941, the Sino-Japanese war became part of the bigger conflict. The Americans sent military aid to Chongqing through Burma but when that route was cut off, the only way in was by air over the Himalayas. The Nationalist government at this point ruled what was known as the Free Zone, incorporating around fifty per cent of the population. In reality, however, its power was limited by how far local provincial authorities supported it.

Chiang, meanwhile, played for time, hoping that the Americans and the Allies would soon bring the Japanese to their knees. By 1941, however, the truce between the communists and the Nationalists was all but over, KMT forces once again attacking Red Army units and blockading Yunan. As the war went on, the morale of the KMT army sank and was not helped by a major famine in China's central provinces in 1943. In 1944, the Japanese defeated a Nationalist army that was about five times larger than their force. This Japanese offensive cut through the centre of China, practically dividing the Nationalist army in two. In May 1945, the war in Europe ended with the defeat of Hitler's Nazi Germany. Meanwhile, things were not going well for the Japanese in the Pacific and in Burma and they now faced the full weight of Allied power. The explosion of atom bombs at Hiroshima and Nagasaki in August 1945 brought a rapid end to hostilities.

The Defeat of the Kuomintang

In China, things returned to normal, with the communists controlling the countryside, but in August 1945 it was hoped that an agreement signed between them and the Nationalists in Chongqing would prevent the resumption of civil war. It was a false hope, however, as neither side was prepared to compromise – the communists would not give up on their army and their aim of land re-distribution; the KMT were vehemently opposed to communism. In terms of support, the KMT's standing had fallen because of Chiang's lack of action against the Japanese. Meanwhile, the communists enjoyed huge support from the mass of ordinary people, the peasants. Only their rich landlords favoured the policies of the KMT. Even in the cities, however, where support for the KMT was usually strong, it had suffered because of corruption and the venality of its officials who had greedily seized banks and businesses following the victory against Japan. This was especially true of the four main families at the top of the KMT – the Chiangs, the Kungs, the Zhens and the Soongs who had become very rich as a result of the war.

The economy was in freefall and inflation rose to dizzy heights. Meanwhile, Chiang's secret police became renowned for their brutality.

The civil war continued with KMT successes in northern China and Manchuria in 1946 and 1947. The city of Yan'an in Shaanxi province was captured as well as all the major cities of Manchuria. As the communists made tactical retreats to preserve their forces and their munitions, the KMT came close to capturing Harbin in Heilongjiang province but a series of offensives led by Lin Biao (1907–71) succeeded in capturing large quantities of weaponry and equipment. These offensives weakened the Nationalists in Manchuria and demoralised their forces. In 1947, the People's Liberation Army (PLA), as the Red Army was now known, rapidly began to gain ground in northern and central China. By March the following year, the Nationalists held only three cities in Manchuria and a month later the communists re-captured Yan'an. Chiang refused to heed advice to pull his troops out of Manchuria and use them to consolidate his position in northern China and in November the last KMT-held city fell. The communists now controlled Manchuria.

Lin Biao moved his troops into the Beijing-Tianjin area, capturing Tianjin on 15th January 1949 and later that month marching into Beijing unopposed. The 200,000 Nationalist troops there joined the People's Liberation Army. Also in January of that year, 300,000 Nationalist troops surrendered near the Huai River, leaving no Nationalist forces north of the Yangtze. The communists offered peace terms which were refused. Nonetheless, Chiang resigned his position as President, being replaced by Li Zongren (1890–1969) who moved the government to Guangzhou. Nanjing and Shanghai fell to the communists in spring of 1949 and Guangzhou was taken in October.

On 10 December 1949, communist forces besieged Chengdu, the last city on mainland China under KMT control. Chiang, once again leader of the Kuomintang, and his son Chiang Ching-kuo (1910–88), later President of the Republic of China, directed operations until they were forced to flee in a plane that conveyed them to the island of Taiwan, taking with them China's gold reserves and many priceless art treasures. Around two million Kuomintang supporters followed them and Chiang Kai-shek never again set foot on mainland China. Things had already moved on, however. On 1 October, speaking in his thick Hunan accent in Beijing's Tiananmen Square, Mao Zedong had proclaimed the establishment of the People's Republic of China.

7. From Radical Reform to Global Superpower

People's Republic of China

China had been at war with itself for almost half a century, engaged in a titanic struggle that, after the First and Second World Wars, was the third biggest conflict in history. It ended with the Chinese Communist Party victorious and now faced with implementing its revolutionary vision. The leaders of the new China were determined not to compromise, embracing the notion of a 'continuing revolution' until the death of Mao Zedong in 1976. They resolved to empower peasants and workers and to take power away from landlords, capitalists, intellectuals and foreigners. The Chinese people were encouraged to embrace change and old ideas and adherence to tradition was discouraged.

The change they embraced was implemented on a massive scale with the construction of schools, hospitals, railways and reservoirs. It came at a cost, however. Everything was politicised and education, the media and even the ability to choose where to live were subject to stringent political control. After all, revolution, as Mao once wrote, was not a genteel practice:

'Revolution is not a dinner party... it cannot be so refined, restrained and magnanimous. A revolution is an insurrection, an act of violence by which one class overthrows another.'
Report on an Investigation into the Peasant Question in Hunan: Mao Zedong, 1927

This became obvious in 1951 when a campaign against 'counter-revolutionaries' resulted in the execution of tens or perhaps even hundreds of thousands while similar numbers were consigned to labour camps.

'Land to the Tillers'

The CCP had already begun to implement its land reform policies three years before its eventual victory in the civil war. It was a hugely popular policy that won it millions of peasant supporters. Landlords' land and property was taken from them and distributed amongst the peasants, each household in a village receiving the same holding. Soon, it was formalised by the new government in the 1950 Agrarian Reform Law. As senior CCP official Liu Shaoqi (1898–1969) explained, the purpose of the new law was not only to end feudal exploitation by landlords, but also to stimulate a rich peasant economy that would encourage the early recovery of agricultural production.

In its initial phase, the Agrarian Reform Law led to some 40 per cent of the land being redistributed and 60 per cent of the Chinese population benefitting from it, women receiving an equal allocation to men. It is estimated that 4.5 million landlords were persecuted or killed, much of this being carried out as part of official campaigns, although Mao had said in 1948 that he envisaged 50 million would 'have to be destroyed' to make the reform happen. It was not a figure that worried him. Some were executed while others were given prison sentences that had an element of farm work that, it was hoped, would re-educate and reform them. Mao himself believed that the people and not security officers should carry out the executions, insisting that their active involvement would permanently link them with the revolutionary process.

For centuries Chinese peasants had dreamed of owning their own plot of land. Mao and the CCP had finally made that dream a reality. There was still much to do, however. The peasant had his own plot but he only had primitive equipment with which to farm it. Furthermore, he remained at the mercy of natural disasters and even illness. If a member of the household fell ill, the reduced labour force might endanger the harvest for that family.

The First Five Year Plan introduced extensive changes to Chinese agriculture, particularly in the way in which it was organised. Farmers were encouraged to work in increasingly large and socialised collective units – cooperative farms. In these collectives, income was based purely on the amount of labour each peasant contributed, rather than on the size of the land they owned. By 1957, about 93.5 per cent of all farming households were members of cooperatives. This shift in working methods also created new outlooks and attitudes amongst the peasant population. Many took on extra, unpaid responsibilities and even management roles when they had no previous experience of such positions, unheard of for peasants in times gone by. Literacy became important as records and accounts had to be kept and reports written. Often, team leaders and other officials were chosen in villages because they could read and write. A leader had to ensure that a decent surplus was produced to serve the needs of the state, but he also had to ensure that his comrades were not discouraged by the amount of their produce they had to give away. This local administration and organisation was also an important development in the Chinese countryside and gave people an opportunity to advance within the party structure, providing unprecedented opportunity for social mobility. The party itself benefitted as membership grew from 2.7 million members in 1947 to 6.1 in 1953 and 17 million in 1961.

The Korean War

Barely had the new government had time to begin implementing its programme than it found itself involved in war in Korea. After the Second World War, the United Nations established a trusteeship administration for Korea, with the USSR administering north of the 38th parallel while the United States administered the south. In 1948, the two sections of the country set up their own governments, establishing the nations of North Korea and South Korea. In June 1950, North Korea invaded its southern neighbour. United States forces, operating under the flag of the United Nations, crossed the 38th parallel in defence of South Korea and advanced on the border between North Korea and China at the Yalu River. China mobilised an army of 'People's Volunteers' under the command of Peng Dehuai (1898–1974) that secretly crossed the river and sprang a surprise attack on the Americans who were forced to retreat south of Seoul.

China sent more than 2.5 million troops to Korea and huge amounts of tanks, artillery and planes but no one came out on top. The war had consequences, however. The Chinese were pleased to have pushed back the 'imperialists' but America now imposed an economic embargo on China and began to provide protection for the Nationalists on Taiwan. The United States became China's number one enemy and all remaining western missionaries, businessmen and consultants were expelled. Relations with the Americans remained bad for many years to come.

It had been an enormously costly war for China just at the time when it was trying to stabilise its economy and re-construct after the civil war. Mao had already been establishing relations with the Soviet Union, declaring his government would 'lean to the east'. Russian leader Joseph Stalin (1878–1953), for his part, was suspicious of the Chinese and their style of Marxism. Mao was frustrated after meeting him shortly after the formation of the People's Republic of China but instead of walking out, his premier, Zhou Enlai, insisted that a formal agreement be signed between the two nations. In February 1950, Mao and Stalin put their names to the Sino-Soviet Treaty of Mutual Friendship. The USSR would provide China with considerable amounts of aid during the 1950s, both economic and in the form of training while many Chinese went to study in Moscow.

Cooling of relations with the USSR and The Great Leap Forward

Relations with the Soviet Union under Nikita Khrushchev (1894–1971) became increasingly strained and the Soviet model of communism became less attractive to Mao and his ministers. The Chinese had been displeased by Khrushchev's denunciation of Stalin in a 1956 speech, Mao considering the former leader a good, well-meaning Marxist. There were many other pressure points in the relationship, principally that Mao felt that the Soviets were not treating China as an equal partner. Furthermore, Khrushchev's approach to the United States was considered too soft by Mao who wanted there to be open hostility with the capitalists. As he once memorably said: 'Do you think the capitalists will put down their butcher knife and become Buddhas?'

A suggestion by Khrushchev of a joint Sino-Soviet fleet was greeted by Mao with suspicion. He insisted that, having driven out the British, the French, the Germans, the Japanese and others, the Chinese would never again allow foreigners on Chinese soil. There were also differences of opinion over Tibet and a failure to support China in its border dispute with India that resulted in the Sino-Indian War of 1962, a conflict won by China. Mao decided, therefore, no longer to follow the Soviet model. It was not providing sufficiently rapid growth, constrained as it was by the use of technical experts and with insufficient capital. What China did have in abundance, of course, was labour.

He announced a Second Five-Year Plan – the 'Great Leap Forward' – a programme designed to use China's vast labour supply to create a rapid increase in agricultural and industrial production. Mao announced the objective of surpassing the steel production of Great Britain by 1968. Huge communes were formed and people were told they would live in an ideal Marxist society where they were divorced totally from ownership of the means of production. In return they were told they would have more schools and hospitals. Small factories – 'backyard steel furnaces' – were created rather than steel mills and locally available materials were used. Women assumed responsibility for the fields while men were marched in military formation to work on public projects such as bridge-, railway- or canal-building. They were fed in mess halls where the food was free. It was claimed that the Great Leap Forward was producing staggering increases in agricultural production.

When veteran revolutionary and minister of defence, Peng Dehuai, mildly criticised the programme at a party meeting in the summer of 1959, Mao was furious and Peng was purged from his position and the party. He and others like him became scapegoats for any problems that were encountered and Peng was later treated with great barbarity during the Cultural Revolution.

There were, indeed, problems. The normal market mechanisms had been disrupted and the goods being produced by the furnaces were of inferior quality. Mistakes, poor planning and a reliance on the government, coupled with the customary natural disasters and unusual weather, led to a devastating famine, even though officials were still reporting increases in production, falsely as it happened. These production rises led the government to take too much of the food supply from the peasants, leaving them, sometimes, with about half of what they needed to live. It has been reported that while people were dying of hunger, there were 22 million tons of grain being held in public granaries. Mao refused to open the doors, claiming that the peasants were hiding grain. Furthermore, he was using grain to pay back some of China's 1.973 billion yen debt to the USSR. Soup kitchens were set up and rationing was practised but it has been estimated that between 20 and 40 million people died of starvation.

During the Great Leap Forward, Chinese rhetoric against the United States reached new levels and they began shelling the islands off the coast of Fujian that were still held by the Nationalists based on Taiwan. The Russians became increasingly concerned that China would drag them into a cataclysmic war with America. In 1959, things got worse when Khrushchev went back on a promise to provide China with atomic weapons and the Soviets cut back on their scientific and technological aid to China. Within a year, they had withdrawn all their personnel, leaving numerous construction projects unfinished. Relations continued to worsen and the Chinese so feared a Russian invasion that huge numbers of air raid shelters were built across the republic. Finally, in 1969 the two powers skirmished several times on the Manchurian border.

The Great Leap Forward did untold damage to China and to Mao Zedong whose stature as a leader and as an economic planner was badly diminished. The peasants were demoralised and this was made even worse by restricted mobility imposed on the Chinese people in 1955. Rural people had to remain in the villages where they were born and women in the villages of their husbands.

Workers sent from the cities to work could not return and peasants were unable, because of the registration system, to go and live in the cities, if they so desired. If a person was not registered in an area, he or she would not have the requisite coupons to obtain grain. It only served to make rural communities even poorer although facilities such as schools and hospitals, as well as food and cheap housing, were plentiful in the cities.

Mao Zedong stepped down from his position as State Chairman of the People's Republic of China in 1959, although he remained Chairman of the CCP. This left Liu Shaoqi – the new PRC Chairman – and Deng Xiaoping (1904–97) – General Secretary of the Communist Party – to manage policy and attempt to bring about economic recovery. In June 1962, amidst a great deal of self-criticism, a conference blamed the disaster of the Great Leap Forward on the cult of personality around Mao Zedong.

The Cultural Revolution

By the mid-1960s, it is easy to see why Mao might have begun to think that his party was pushing him to one side while Liu Shaoqi, Chen Yun (1905–95), Zhou Enlai and Deng Xiaoping made all the important decisions. Mao began to fear that his revolution was going the way of most others – a new elite was rising up to replace the old one. He only needed to look at the Soviet Union to see what had happened to their revolution. Mao believed that revolution was an ongoing process of unending class struggle. He also wished to see his enemies within the CCP and in the country identified and dealt with. For these reasons, in 1966, he called for a Great Revolution to Create a Proletarian Culture. In so doing, he created a movement that for the next decade would rip out the heart of China and almost destroy the party to which Mao had devoted himself for the past thirty years.

He prepared the ground in the spring of 1966 when a number of officials in Beijing were purged, including Mayor Peng Zhen (1902–97) who was denounced for allowing a play to be staged – *Hai Rui Dismissed from Office* – that was critical of Mao. Before long, handwritten posters appeared in places like Beijing University, denouncing senior officials such as Liu and Deng for 'taking the capitalist road'. Well-known officials suddenly disappeared from view to be replaced by unknowns. Mao's wife Jiang Qing (1914–91) and her associates, later to be dubbed the 'Gang of Four', became prominent in the movement and it was surmised that, never having taken a political role before, she was now acting as a mouthpiece for her husband around whom an even greater personality cult grew.

The students who took part in the Cultural Revolution were named Red Guards and, on 18 August, approximately 11 million of them turned up in Tiananmen Square to listen to Mao and Lin Biao praise their actions. Badges, posters and pictures of Mao were everywhere and his youthful followers clutched copies of *Quotations from Chairman Mao*, known in the West as *The Little Red Book*. They were unfailing in their loyalty. One group of Red Guards swore this oath, for instance:

> 'We are Chairman Mao's Red Guard, and Chairman Mao is our highest leader... We have unlimited trust in the people! We have the deepest hatred for our enemies! In life, we struggle for the party! In death, we give ourselves up for the benefit of the people!... With our blood and our lives, we swear to defend Chairman Mao! Chairman Mao, we have unlimited faith in you!'
> Red Guard quotations: Song Yianyi et al. (eds.) *Chinese Cultural Revolution Database* (Hong Kong, 2002)

The Cultural Revolution was a genuinely mass political movement with widespread support. It was violent, anti-intellectual and xenophobic, accusing teachers and experts of putting their expertise and intellect before their credentials as revolutionaries. It was also a response to Mao Zedong's conviction that the CCP had grown soft and had become too interested in urban matters, neglecting its roots. It spread like wildfire and not even Mao or Jiang could control it. The Red Guards took action against anything foreign or old, destroying art treasures, old books, temples and mosques. Writers and teachers were denounced by their friends in public as former colleagues jeered at them.

In July 1967, it escalated into an armed struggle as various Red Guard factions and workers' groups began to fight each other as well as Chinese regional and national military forces. The country came to a standstill and the shops emptied of merchandise. Fearing that China was on the verge of full-scale civil war, Mao disbanded the Red Guards in July 1968, sending them to work in the fields. The terror was not over, however, because the army took over the search for traitors. Thousands were tortured and executed, for instance, during the investigation into the May 16 Group conspiracy. The involvement of the military declined, however, following the bizarre death of Lin Biao, Mao's minister of defence, in 1971. Lin, who had been a devoted student of Mao, became convinced that his leader had turned against him, and decided to assassinate him. When the plot was exposed, Lin boarded a plane to flee to the Soviet Union. Carrying insufficient fuel, the plane crashed in Mongolia. Mao managed to keep news of Lin's fall from grace out of the media for a year but mystery still surrounds the incident.

Jiang Qing remained as leader of the radical faction, protecting Chinese revolutionary culture against revisionist ideas. She was opposed by the more moderate Zhou Enlai who was preoccupied with foreign affairs, especially China's abiding fear throughout the Cultural Revolution of an invasion by the Soviet Union. He arranged the momentous visit of United States President Richard Nixon (1913–1994) to China in 1972 during which the diplomatic agreement known as the Shanghai Communiqué was signed. The following year he managed the reinstatement to senior posts of many of the disgraced officials, including Deng Xiaoping. Zhou, who had been China's premier since the revolution, died of cancer in January 1976. Those who paid their respects to him in Tiananmen Square were branded 'counter-revolutionary' by Jiang Qing and her associates and attempts to suppress the mourning led to a riot. She ensured that Deng was purged again.

On the afternoon of 9 September 1976, it was announced that Mao Zedong had died and China descended into mourning, people weeping openly in the streets and public institutions closing for a week. Hua Guofeng (1921–2008), a Mao loyalist from Hunan, was his designated successor both as the paramount leader of the Communist Party of China and the People's Republic of China. On 6 October, Hua brought the Cultural Revolution to an end and, to the delight of most Chinese people, ordered the arrest of the Gang of Four – Jiang Qing, Zhang Chunqiao (1917–2005), Yao Wenyuan (1931–2005) and Wang Hongwen (1935–92). At a show trial in 1980–81, they were found guilty of anti-party activities. Jiang and Zhang were sentenced to death but their sentences were commuted to life imprisonment; Wang was sentenced to life imprisonment; and Yao got twenty years.

The China left behind by the Gang of Four and the Cultural Revolution was badly damaged. The young people who had been sent out to the countryside felt as much victims as the people they had persecuted; the education of a generation had been seriously disrupted and those who had been beaten and humiliated found themselves working alongside their persecutors, an invidious situation that dragged on for years. Mao's standing was further damaged by the dreadful acts of those years. After his death, he was still revered for his leadership during the civil war but there is little doubt that much of the blame for all that went wrong from the mid–1950s onwards can be laid at his door. Some describe him as a megalomaniac, a monster who tried to re-fashion China according to his will, regardless of the cost in terms of lives. Others maintain that to describe him thus merely absolves everyone else of responsibility.

Renewal, Reform and Reaching Out

Within two years of assuming power, Hua Guofeng was outmanoeuvred by the wily survivor, Deng Xiaoping. When he arrived at the top of the party, Deng was less concerned by ideology and the class struggle than he was by the pressing problem of poverty in China. This, despite the fact that he had been a revolutionary just as long as Chairman Mao, having worked with Zhou Enlai in France in the 1920s and having participated in the Shanghai underground, the Long March and guerrilla activity against the Japanese invaders. Apart from his two ejections during the

Cultural Revolution, he had been a member of the Politburo – the executive committee of the CCP – since 1956. Although he never held office as head of state, head of government or General Secretary of the Communist Party, he was, nonetheless, paramount leader of China from 1978 to 1992. His astonishing political comeback brought a programme that was radically different to that of Mao Zedong.

In 1953, life expectancy had been forty, reaching sixty by 1968 and sixty-five by 1984, largely due to public health improvements started in the 1950s. This led to rapid population growth, China's population topping the billion mark by the mid-1970s. As Deng realised, economic growth, following the damage that had been done by the Cultural Revolution, was essential in order to feed this expanding population. He introduced the 'Four Modernisations', a slogan originally coined by Zhou Enlai. The four elements of the economy to which he referred were agriculture, industry, science and technology and national defence. The initial step was the dismantling of the collective farms, with farmers being permitted to sell a proportion of their crops in the free market. Small enterprises were encouraged, 12 million of them being registered by 1985. Efforts at economic equality were abandoned, Deng proudly declaring 'To get rich is glorious'. Four Special Economic Zones were set up on the Chinese coast, aimed at obtaining foreign investment. He even supported the introduction of joint ventures between foreign firms and Chinese government agencies, the low labour costs proving particularly attractive to foreigners. Factories were set up to produce consumer goods for the West and areas such as Guangdong, with its quick access to Hong Kong's financial power and the special economic zone established at Shenzen, did particularly well. People began to prosper and acquire the trappings of modern prosperity such as pagers and mobile phones. These steps showed dividends, China enjoying an astonishing economic boom that trebled average incomes by the early 1990s. The World Bank reported that a staggering 170 million Chinese peasants had been moved out of poverty.

China was still a long way from what one protester called the

'Fifth Modernisation' – democracy – but there was certainly a great deal more openness than under Mao. Hu Yaobang (1915–89), an often-purged survivor like Deng who served on the Politburo, encouraged a greater level of debate in journals and think tanks. China even established diplomatic relations with the United States and foreign tourists were allowed into the country, arriving in droves, while many young Chinese people went abroad to study. Indeed, education was the object of a great deal of attention as China attempted to make up lost ground in science and technology. But it remained tied to its founding values as Deng proved when he introduced the 'Four Cardinal Principals' – retaining the socialist path; the dictatorship of the proletariat; the leadership of the Communist Party and the ideology of Marxism, Leninism and Maoism.

Nonetheless, the new freedoms led to a desire for even more and student protests in 1985–6 led to the resignation of the relatively liberal Hu Yaobang. In April 1989, when Hu died, student protests against the pervasive role of the CCP in everyday life erupted across China. In spring of that year, Tiananmen Square was the scene of unprecedented protests in which the participants demanded 'science and democracy'. Almost a million Chinese students and workers thronged in the space in front of the Gate of Heavenly Peace, all of it recorded by television cameras to the huge embarrassment of the Chinese government, especially as the world's media had gathered for another important event – the visit of the Soviet leader, Mikhail Gorbachev (b. 1931).

By June, there were still several thousand immovable demonstrators in the square but on the night of 3 June, the authorities struck, sending in tanks and armoured personnel carriers. It is likely that many hundreds lost their lives that night but the official death tally has never been made public. There were hundreds of arrests and many fled to the West to escape incarceration. At the end of the protests, however, it appeared that the hardliners had come out on top and the cries for science and democracy had been silenced.

Third and Fourth Generations

Tiananmen Square did not have the cataclysmic consequences that some feared – civil war or the end of reform. Certainly the liberal trends of the late 1980s that had led to the demonstrations were brought to an end – the 'evil winds of bourgeois liberalism' as they were called. By 1992, Deng, now 88 years old, had chosen a successor. He was Jiang Zemin (b. 1926), the Mayor of Shanghai, a man who had dealt with the 1989 protests more effectively than the authorities in Beijing. General Secretary of the party since 1989, he was anointed leader in 1992 at the Fourteenth Party Congress, retaining that position at the Fifteenth Congress in 1997. He was the first of a new generation of leaders, demonstrating the demise of the peasant revolutionaries and the arrival of well-educated, professional technocrats at the top.

In the three years after the Tiananmen Square protests, China had become a pariah to the rest of the international community. The hardliners had begun to place restrictions on China's burgeoning free enterprise and propaganda and ideology campaigns had returned, although the Chinese public at large paid them little attention. As communist governments fell around the world, however, the CCP remained firmly in control. In 1992, Deng Xiaoping re-emerged to make a tour of southern China and renew the push for a market-orientated economy, a clarion call that was endorsed at the Fourteenth Party Congress later that year. His legacy has been astonishing. Since his death, under the leadership of his successor, Jiang, China has sustained an annual growth in GDP of 8 per cent, achieving one of the world's highest rates per capita economic growth. Astonishingly, China became the world's fastest growing major economy.

In 1993, when he was elected president, Jiang coined the new term 'socialist market economy' to take China's centrally planned socialist economy into what would essentially be a government-regulated capitalist market economy – another step in the direction of Deng Xiaoping's 'Socialism with Chinese characteristics'. Shanghai, once the engine room of China's industry, commerce and culture, was given permission to throw its doors wide open to foreign investment. By 1998, Jiang had reversed Deng's policy of separating Party governance, government and the military and assumed the positions of CCP General Secretary, President of the People's Republic of China and Chairman of the Central Military Commission, centralising power in one man again, thus stabilising the country and its institutions. As the new century approached, China's economy bucked every trend. Its GDP still continued to grow despite the 1997 Asian Financial Crisis and catastrophic flooding of the Yangtze in 1998. As foreign investment halved worldwide in 2000, it rose by 10 per cent in China, companies around the world anxious not to miss out on the Chinese boom.

In July 1997, after lengthy negotiations, sovereignty over Hong Kong, one of the world's top financial centres, was transferred from the United Kingdom to China after the expiry of its 99-year lease, ending 156 years of British colonial rule. Macau, a former Portuguese colony, was also handed over. Both retained a form of governance over their own affairs and kept independent economic, social and justice systems.

Although it is believed that Jiang wished to carry on, he stepped down from the Politburo and his position as General Secretary of the Communist Party in 2002, making way for Hu Jintao (b. 1942), a representative of China's 'Fourth Generation' of political leaders and the first without any revolutionary credentials. Hu succeeded Jiang as President on 15 March 2003. Involved in Communist Party bureaucracy for much of his life, Hu and his prime minister Wen Jiabao (b. 1942) inherited a government blighted by corruption – yes, some things never change – and a country experiencing an astonishing increase in materialism. Indeed, according to opinion polls, corruption is the number one priority of the Chinese people who come up against it in almost every sector of society – hospitals, schools, police and social and legal institutions. There are those who claim that the authorities are reluctant to pursue senior figures. Punishment in such cases, therefore, takes the form of purging from the party rather than legal sanction. There have been changes, however. For instance, during the SARS epidemic of 2002 to 2003, as the world focused on China, classified data regarding the epidemic was made public and officials who had made administrative errors stepped down from their positions. Hu even made a high-profile trip to Guangdong while Wen ate lunch with students at Beijing University to allay fears.

The new government made efforts to help Chinese farmers, still representing more than 50 per cent of the Chinese population. In an unprecedented move, all taxation on farming was abolished in 2005. Efforts have also been made to reduce rural poverty and China's poverty rate has fallen below 10 per cent, while literacy now exceeds 95 per cent. Control of the media was initially loosened, but the government still retains the power to dismiss reporters or close down newspapers that do not adhere to party guidelines. The Internet, however, has provided problems for the Chinese authorities. Reluctant to give their people unbridled access and the opportunity to express negative critical opinion about the PRC, they have introduced a range of laws and regulations – known as the 'Great Firewall of China' – that make China the most repressed advanced country in the world in terms of Internet access. Indeed, Amnesty International has described China as having 'the largest recorded number of imprisoned journalists and cyber-dissidents in the world'. Website content is routinely blocked and the Internet access of individuals is closely monitored by an Internet police force estimated to number around 30,000.

Vastly improved healthcare has resulted in a number of diseases disappearing and, in the coming years, China expects to wipe out leprosy and iodine deficiency. After exploding during the rule of Mao Zedong, the population has stabilised, partly due to the lower birth rate that has resulted from the one child policy instituted in the PRC in 1978. This policy is estimated by the Chinese authorities to have prevented more than 400 million births. As a result of such steps, life expectancy has risen to 72 years of age; in 1940, it had been 40 years of age. In 2009, the population of China was estimated at 1,346,227,885.

Epilogue: China at the Crossroads

By 2012, according to the International Monetary Fund, China was the world's second-largest economy, in terms of nominal GDP, and its economy is almost a hundred times greater than it was at the launch of economic liberalisation in 1978. It is now the world's fastest-growing economy and its second-largest trading power behind only the United States, its 2011 international trade value totaling US$3.64 trillion. Astonishingly, between 2007 and 2011, its economic growth was equivalent to the growth of all the G7 countries combined.

A number of factors, several of which are the subject of some controversy, have contributed to these staggering figures. Firstly, China has an almost inexhaustible supply of cheap labour and hundreds of millions of people have re-located from the countryside to the cities to work long hours in factories for low wages. Productivity is high and the country's infrastructure is good. The government is favourable to industry and investment but, critically, China enjoys an exchange rate that many believe to be undervalued, a matter of dispute between China and its major trading partners.

It is felt, however, that the economic model that has provided China with three decades of double-digit growth is beginning to flag, providing difficult choices for the country's fifth-generation leader, Xi Jingping (born 1953), appointed at the 18th National Congress of the Communist Party of China in November 2012. What seems inescapable is the fact that there must be change if a predicted fall in growth is to be avoided. Many analysts believe that there has to be a bigger role, for instance, for the private sector and that consumer spending should be encouraged, moving away from China's reliance on exports and investment. These are changes that will, however, be staunchly resisted by powerful vested interests within the Chinese Communist Party and the state-owned companies that have enjoyed special treatment for so long.

The current economic model has created dangerous social tensions within China and is responsible for a society that suffers from one of the widest gaps between rich and poor in Asia. Services are notoriously poor, although the government has been attempting to tackle these issues with an expansion of education and in the provision of health insurance. There is still a great deal to be done, however, especially by cash-strapped local governments. An ageing population adds to the problems, and the unpopular one-child policy means that there are fewer working young people to provide taxes to pay for those in retirement. Meanwhile, China is home to sixteen of the world's twenty most polluted cities and the environment is becoming a major issue. Examples of tree planting and improvements in urban sewage treatment demonstrate efforts to deal with these problems but they are by no means adequate and may, for the foreseeable future, be sacrificed to the desire of the Chinese people for new cars, new homes and consumer goods.

Many critics blame the one-party system for China's mounting problems, insisting that in order to progress the country must become more democratic. High-profile activists such as the artist Ai Weiwei (born 1957) continue to risk a great deal by expressing criticism of the leadership but there is no interest in political reform or democracy at the top. They are focused instead on the economy and social stability and must hope that they can stimulate continued growth. To this end, the next decade will be critical. If they fail, it may be time for the Chinese people to rise up and effect change, not for the first time in their long and fascinating history.

Further Reading

Dikötter, Frank, *Mao's Great Famine: The History of China's Most Devastating Catastrophe, 1958–62*, Bloomsbury: London, 2011

Ebrey, Patricia Buckley, *The Cambridge Illustrated History of China*, Cambridge: Press Syndicate of the University of Cambridge, 1996

Fenby, Jonathan, *The Penguin History of Modern China: The Fall and Rise of a Great Power, 1850–2009*, Penguin: London, 2009

Gascoigne, Bamber, *A Brief History of the Dynasties of China*, Robinson Publishing: London, 2003

Keay, John, *China: A History*, London, HarperPress, 2009

Kruger, Rayne, *All Under Heaven: A Complete History of China*, Wiley, Chichester, 2003

Mitter, Rana, *Modern China: A Very Short Introduction*, Oxford University Press: Oxford, 2008

Paludan, Ann, *Chronicle of the Chinese Emperors*, Thames & Hudson: London, 1998

Roberts, J.A.G., *The Complete History of China*, Stroud: Sutton, 2003

Roberts, J.A.G., *A History of China*, Palgrave: London, 2006

Index